WHERE ARE YOU MY CHILD?

Aliza Ramati

Zaccmedia

Published by Zaccmedia
www.zaccmedia.com
info@zaccmedia.com

English edition published in the United Kingdom in 2015

This edition copyright © 2015 by Anne Heelis, Nachamu Ami. The moral rights of the author, Aliza Ramati, have been asserted.

Email: nachamuami@btinternet.com

All rights reserved. No part of this publication may be reproduced, stored in a retrieval system, or transmitted in any form or by any means, electronic, mechanical, photocopying or otherwise, without the prior written permission of the publisher.

Original Hebrew edition published with the assistance of
Keren Havatzelet – Culture and Education Institutions
©All rights reserved by the author and by Moreshet Publishing House-
Mordechai Anielevich Memorial and Research Center
POB 40009, Tel Aviv 61400, Israel
www.moreshet.org
Email: moreshet@kba.org.il
Hebrew edition ISBN: 978-965-7026-81-6
Hebrew edition printed in Israel by 'Seder Tzalam', Tel Aviv 2009

Translated into English by Rebecca Loveall. Email: freshair1@gmail.com

The following images are reproduced with kind permission of the Avri & Simcha Rosenfeld Collection, Kfar Ruppin, Israel: Images on pages 82, 87, 90, 128

Images are sourced from the original Hebrew edition, and all effort has been made in good faith to locate the original copyright owners. Should any issue arise over the usage of any images included, please contact the publisher who will where necessary remove any image that is not permitted for usage.

British Library Cataloguing-in-Publication Data
A catalogue record for this book is available from the British Library.

Cover design: Zaccmedia

ISBN 978-1-909824-79-9

Contents

Introduction to the English Publication   v
Dedication   vii
Author's Introduction   viii
Shalom to You, Dear Readers!   x

1. The Mystery Suitcase   1
2. Great-grandfather was Right   6
3. Koppel and the Clarinet   11
4. Love at First Sight   17
5. Secrets I Must Find Out   20
6. Arguments and a Wedding   24
7. Farewell   30
8. A Letter   32
9. Fear and Joy   37
10. The Covenant   42
11. In the Transit Camp   45
12. Birth   50
13. Three Babies   54
14. Chaim, Sheindele, a Baby and an Aunt   57
15. At Last   63
16. Setting Out   68
17. Hard, Hard, Hard   72

18. Frustrating Questions	75
19. The Sea is Against Us Too	77
20. The Ship Gets Stuck	83
21. Dreams and a Surprise	88
22. Sights of the City of Haifa… and also Oranges	93
23. Prepare for Tomorrow	100
24. The Mandate Government Wins Again	106
25. Rut, and a British Officer	111
26. A Bitter Day	116
27. Bilhah, My Angel	119
28. Mauritius	124
29. Malaria, and a Letter	129
30. Good Siblings and Uncle Yoav	135
31. The Mystery of the Pacifier and the Scar	143
32. First Home in the Homeland	149
33. Annina	152
34. A New Identity	155
35. Petr	162
36. Simon	170
Glossary	174

Introduction to the English Publication

In November 2013 Hatikvah Film Trust arranged the premier screening of the Hebrew version of *The Forsaken Promise* documentary film at the Menachem Begin Heritage Center in Jerusalem. This film exposes Britain's failure to keep the pledge made in the Balfour Declaration of 1917 and to carry out her legal obligations under the Mandate. The event was supported by Love Never Fails, which is a group of Christian organizations in the United Kingdom, promoting a biblical understanding of God's continuing faithfulness to and purposes for Israel and encouraging repentance for past actions towards the Jewish people. The invited audience of about three hundred included those who suffered as a result of Britain's actions, and British people visiting or living in Israel.

In his speech after the screening of the film, the producer, Hugh Kitson, expressed the very real sense of sorrow and shame felt by thousands of Christians in Britain over our nation's betrayal of the Jewish people during the Mandate. This betrayal resulted in the deaths of an untold number of Jewish people who were unable to escape the Nazi Holocaust and enter their ancient Promised Land, which they should have been free to do under the terms of the Mandate. Towards the end of his speech, Mr Kitson said that today there are thousands of Jewish people who have a grievance with

Britain over our betrayal of their people. Then he added, 'As a British citizen, and on behalf of Love Never Fails and the British Christians who are here with us tonight, I want to say "sorry" to you all. WE say sorry to you all.'

Aliza Ramati, the author of this book, and her husband Gidon, were among the guests that evening and she had an important conversation with Rosie Ross, the Love Never Fails representative in Israel. Aliza asked for help to translate this book from the original Hebrew into English. It was felt we could not refuse this request and Nachamu Ami (one of the members of Love Never Fails) took on the task of having the book translated and published in English. It is our desire that the story of the suffering of one Jewish family during the time of the British Mandate will give more understanding about this dark part of our history.

Signed:

Hugh Kitson, Hatikvah Films
www.hatikvah.co.uk

Rosie Ross, Repairing the Breach
rosses@netvision.net.il

Anne Heelis, Nachamu Ami
nachamuami@btinternet.com

Date: February 2015

Dedication

To our parents, the heroes.

To my husband, who rose from the sea, spread his wings and was victorious.

To our dear children, who gave us rooted grandchildren, who give us the true meaning of life and fill our hearts with hope.

Aliza Ramati

Author's Introduction

The story set out here is that of the phoenix, rising from the ashes.

My dear family members are involved in it: my husband, his parents and their acquaintances.

From these pages I wish to bring our children and their families to meet with the time of the *ha'apala*, the illegal immigration, and shed light on it.

Thanks to my husband's parents, who had time to tell us what happened to them before they passed away.

Great thanks to my husband, Gidi, who shared with me all he knew and all he heard from his parents.

Heartfelt thanks to David Yosef Adler, a broad-horizoned man with great knowledge, whose memoirs are a witness of the life in Czechoslovakia, the *hachshara* and the detention camp in Mauritius, and who passed on to me what he wrote. To my sorrow, David Yosef passed away during the writing and I will miss him greatly.

Thanks to the Illegal Immigration Museum in Atlit and especially to Ms Naomi Yitzhar, who sent me documents and photos.

Lastly, thanks to Bilhah Luz, my good friend, who assisted me greatly during the writing.

So that we do not forget the hundreds who were sacrificed during the *ha'apala*, so that we protect what we have here, we must write, tell, and remind us all.

And always, after winter, the spring comes.

Aliza

Shalom to You, Dear Readers!

My name is Roni. I'm an Israeli girl in middle school, and live in a cooperative village called a moshav. [A moshav is like a kibbutz, but cooperative to a lesser degree.] There's a big garden around my house, and most of the important things happen there. I run wild in it with my brother and sisters – with Shiri, who is also my best friend and who's already in the third form; with Rotem, my brother, who is very mischievous, and with tiny Tali. I know how to do cartwheels and to stand on my head for a really long time. Grandma asks me if I go to school like that...

I know everyone thinks their mother is the best in the world, but I'm sure Ima really is. My father is a career officer in the army. For many days he is absent from home, and when he comes, we all pounce on him. Rotem climbs on him and sits on his shoulders, jumps and prances around him, and so does Tali, my baby sister, but he is free for me and my sister Shiri only after the younger children are already asleep and the house is quiet. Mowgli the dog and Tuli, our impertinent cat, are also happy when Abba comes.

Our grandparents live next door, and that's really fun. They spoil us and tell us exciting stories. But recently I've been very busy. The teacher has given everyone in the class a very serious assignment, an assignment that's forced me to find out many secrets. Since then I've become a real detective. I ask, search, gather information from here and there and try to solve mysteries.

The story I'm going to tell has many unknowns: a bedraggled pacifier, a scar, photos of people wearing strange clothing; even the names of the people in this story sound strange. I have found letters written in an unknown language, and there are many words I need to learn the meaning of.

If you're ready, we'll start with solving the first mystery, the one I've been trying to solve since the fifth form. I've already found a clue.

Roni, with her grandparents, Gidon and Aliza Ramati (June 2015)

1
The Mystery Suitcase

It's already afternoon. The sun is getting ready to go to bed, and wrapping itself in colourful, soft clouds. Our sun loves pink sheets. Sometimes it covers itself in red sheets. I love to look at it as it's getting ready for bed. I stand on the path by Grandma's house, the highest place in the village, and look to the west. The sky is painted with awesome colours. And then, when the sun is covered, I start yawning. I feel like curling up in my soft blanket.

Today I come to Grandpa Gidi and Grandma Aliza's house straight from school. They wait for me with lunch, but Grandma doesn't sit with me. She is busy. She and Grandpa have decided to refurbish their house, and almost all its contents are outside. Boxes, furniture, books, albums and everything. Grandma has asked me to help and pack all the albums from the cupboard into a box.

I pack quickly. I put the big albums in the bottom, and the smaller albums above. Grandpa helps me to close the box and seal it with tape. I write 'Albums' on the box with a thick marker, and go on to an empty one. There's a lot more to pack.

At the bottom of the cupboard I see a small suitcase. It looks tattered, and its brown colour is faded. Our shiny suitcases at home even have wheels, but this one looks really old. Its corners are worn completely, and it is marked with the name 'Grinfeld' in white letters.

'Grandpa, who is Grinfeld?' I ask Grandpa Gidi.

'Grinfeld is my parents' name, Reiseleh and Mittyu. This suitcase is theirs.'

Grandpa Gidi sinks deep in thought. He is silent for a while, and suddenly finds out that I'm waiting for an answer.

'*Nu*, what do you want to know? How this suitcase got here? Do you remember your great-grandparents, Reiseleh and Mittyu, my parents?'

'Not very well. I remember Grandma Reiseleh had blue eyes, and always sang strange songs to me in a strange language. They had a cassette player that always played nice music, and sometimes Grandpa would change the reel. He loved to record music, and was always recording or listening. I also remember Grandpa Mittyu in shorts, going from tree to tree with a garden hose, and I went and watered with him, till I got completely wet and Ima had to change all my clothes. I still sleep on the bed Grandpa Mittyu made for me. So what's this suitcase, Grandpa?'

'Roni, my parents, Reiseleh and Mittyu, looked for it for a long time. They used to say that they were looking for their past. Yes, this is the suitcase of their past.'

'I remember that Grandpa Mittyu got sick and passed away a few years ago. I even remember Grandma Reiseleh being sad. Soon afterwards she too died.'

Grandpa Gidi has blue eyes. I look for the smile in his eyes, but he looks thoughtful.

'So why did they look for this suitcase?' I ask. 'And how does the name "Grinfeld" belong to them at all?'

'Grandma and Grandpa used to go back and visit the kibbutz that was our first home in Israel. They continued to look for the lost suitcase, but didn't find it.'

'How did they lose it?'

'They put it on a lorry with all the possessions they had, after they had decided to move from Kibbutz Gvar'am to the village. On the way the side of the lorry came loose, and many items were scattered over the exit road from the kibbutz. The lorry stopped, they got off and put back all the possessions that had fallen off, but when they unpacked everything in their new home in the village, they didn't find the suitcase. Since then, each time they went to the kibbutz on a visit they would ask if someone had found the tattered suitcase. But, to their disappointment, no one found it and no one heard of it.'

Grandpa is quiet, and closes his eyes. Tiny wrinkles like the folds of a little fan decorate them from the outside. Then he opens his eyes and gives me a loving glance.

'After my mother passed away,' he goes on, 'a friend from the kibbutz came to comfort us. He was already very old. His name was Shaul, and he was a good friend of Ima's and Abba's. He held a small suitcase in his hand. I remembered it immediately, as soon as I saw it. This was the suitcase my parents had wanted to find so badly. I asked him where he had found it, and Shaul told me the whole story: a year beforehand he had been given the task of establishing an archive in the kibbutz. A month before he had been sitting in one of the storage sheds in the kibbutz and rummaging through a pile of junk and castaway items. It was there that he found the suitcase with Grinfeld written on it.

'"I decided to bring the suitcase to you, Gidi. It's too bad that your parents didn't see the lost item coming back to them," he said sadly.'

When Grandpa Gidi finishes telling, a long silence falls between us. He holds the suitcase on his knees and strokes it tenderly, and then puts it back in its place.

What's so exciting about an old, battered suitcase? I wonder, but don't say it aloud. 'But Grandpa, why does it say Grinfeld on it? It's not your name, or your parents' name either?'

'Ronchu, it's hard to explain things to you now, and in any case, you don't need to know everything in one day. When you grow up, I promise I'll tell you everything, everything...'

These answers annoy me most. When they want me to be grown, I'm grown. When they're uncomfortable, I'm still a child. But I'll investigate. I will find the answer. I go to the suitcase and open it without permission. I find a tin in it. Hmm, what treasure is in this tin? I open it as well. There are many pages in it, rolled like a scroll and tied with a ribbon. I take off the ribbon. Pages, yellowed with age, with an unclear handwriting on them... There is an envelope in the tin as well. I pick it up, and an old, tattered, white pacifier falls out of it.

'What, don't you have anything else you want to keep?' I want to throw the envelope with the pacifier into the trash, but Grandpa Gidi notices and stops me.

'Roni,' he says, 'you're not to throw anything away. This pacifier has a story.'

'Grandpa, you must be joking. Actually, you know what, maybe you'll tell me a story for once? Tell me the story of the pacifier.'

'I promise I'll tell you, but not today. Don't be angry. I'm tired.'

I sit by the table, put the pages on it, and spread them out carefully. I can't understand the writing, but from the order of the lines it looks like these are letters. I go back to the suitcase. There are a few other things in it, like a big album. The cover is faded. Once it was blue. I leaf through it. The album has many old papers and photos, pictures of people wearing strange clothes. I go back to the letters and try to read them, but without success.

'Grandpa, what is this album?'

Grandpa takes the album out of my hands.

'Ronchu,' so Grandpa calls me, 'this album is old, and needs to be treated with respect. This is your great-grandparents' album.'

2
Great-grandfather was Right

Now I'm already 13 and in the eighth form, and we've been given a 'roots' assignment. Our teacher, Yonit, tells us that what is interesting in these assignments is the stories that Grandma and Grandpa tell, stories about the land of their birth, their childhood, their parents and siblings, their immigration to Israel – *aliyah*, if they weren't born here, of course, and if possible, it would be best to attach pictures, letters, maps and so on.

I immediately remember the brown suitcase, the big album with the old cover, the wrinkled letters, the strange photos and the pacifier. Now Grandma and Grandpa won't be able to get away. They'll have to tell me.

When I come into their house I am grinning. I give Grandpa and Grandma each a hug, and say, 'Well, then...'

Grandma understands. 'Roni, you want a story? You're a bit old for Grandma's stories, aren't you?'

'You know, Grandma, we learned a song today. Maybe you know it too?' I start to sing. 'Tell me, tell me a tale, about those days, about what is past...' Grandma joins me, 'Exaggerate greatly, my grandmother, how do you say "ghost story" in Hebrew?'

I give Grandma a big hug. 'While I eat, you get ready. Today you have to tell me an especially long story. I need it for the "roots" assignment. So...'

'"Roots" assignment? That would take years! Ronchu, we can't finish that in one day. We'll start tomorrow, all right? I'll organize the material in my head, we'll sit comfortably and talk."

When I get home, I immediately do my homework. I free up time for tomorrow. I make a special notebook, write a table of contents for the paper, and wait impatiently for tomorrow to come.

'So where should we start?' Grandma asks.

Grandma and Grandpa sit opposite me, looking at me with a loving, soft look. This is the look that gives me much strength.

'Grandma, start from... from wherever you want. I'll listen and we'll decide together where to start. I know the beginning is hard, but afterwards I'm sure everything will flow quickly.'

'All right, well... you know, Roni, great things really did happen to our parents. In fact, if we're talking about roots, we need to dig deep. How about we start from... do you remember the old blue album? You'll find "roots" there. Page through it carefully, try to organize things for yourself, and write down questions. We'll do our best to answer every question you ask.'

Now I'm alone in Grandma and Grandpa's study. The blue album is on the desk. I turn the pages carefully, so that they don't fall apart. The pictures are faded. I notice a white page that is relatively new. I recognize Grandpa Gidi's handwriting. A clear handwriting. I can read this. It's in Hebrew. This is the eulogy that Grandpa read over his parents' graves at the one-year anniversary of their death. I was little then, maybe six years old, but I remember the tears and the last words of what Grandpa had read: 'We are living here, my dear father, because you were right.'

Grandpa Gidi's voice had cracked as he said these words. Grandma Aliza cried too, and so had my mother, Chagit, and Aunt Naama, and Uncle Yoav had wiped a tear away from under his dark glasses.

I hold the eulogy that Grandpa Gidi read then and try to understand things, but I don't understand anything.

My father and mother,

> I can't talk about you, Father, or about you, Mother, separately. You were always together. Shared everything. You lived together for sixty-four years. Since that meeting in the *hachshara* agricultural training of the 'Young Pioneer' movement in Karpathoros in Czechoslovakia. Together you came to the Land, together...

I skip over what's written and get to the end of the eulogy. My eyes are filled with tears.

> You were a big family there, in distant Karpathoros, and only you were left, of all the many relatives. Most of the family remained 'there'. Died in the concentration camps. You were left, because you were right. So your mother said, my dear father, before she jumped from the train to her death. We heard about it from an acquaintance who survived. She said to him before she jumped: Mittyu was right.

> You were right, Father. We live because you were right.

What was he right about?

I try to reconstruct how Grandpa Mittyu and Grandma Reiseleh looked. I close my eyes tightly and try to remember them. Two old, beautiful people. They loved me so much. I remember myself sitting in Grandma Reiseleh's lap and listening to the song she sang to me in that unknown language. I remember Grandpa Mittyu gathering nuts with me under the pecan tree in their yard. Grandpa called Grandma Reiseleh 'my hero'. Why did he call her that?

'You were right.'

What was my great-grandfather right about?

Grandma sees me absorbed in reading. She strokes my hair, gives me a plateful of fruit and says, 'Ronchu, maybe you should rest now? Come, sit with us. You can go on afterwards.'

Grandma doesn't understand that I can't stop. I ask for permission to take this big album home. At home I can sit with it whenever I have time. I can read and organize things.

Grandma puts the album carefully in a big envelope.

'Roni, guard the album. Especially from Rotem, your brother. He doesn't take care yet with things like this.'

'Grandma, what else, other than the album, was in that suitcase you put in the storage attic during the renovations? You know, the old suitcase that has "Grinfeld" on it?'

'Roni, even we haven't been able to check everything in it yet. There are many letters there that are hard to read. And we don't understand Czech.'

That night I sit with Ima. My brother and sisters are already asleep. Now, at last, Ima has time to be alone with me. I know she's very tired. Abba won't come home tonight either. He's in the army, and he has lots of work we don't talk about at home. When Abba's with the army, Ima has to do everything herself. But she still finds time to be with me. I love to share with her what is going on with me, and she always listens, even though she's tired.

I tell Ima about the assignment we've been given to write a 'roots' paper. I also have an exam in two days, and lots of homework, and each teacher thinks the homework they give is the most important, as though we have nothing else to do in life. Now this paper has been added, and it needs to be well-rounded, with maps, and pictures, and postcards, and letters, and...

The album in my lap falls with a *thunk*. I bend down to pick it up. A picture falls out. I look at this picture and see an older man holding two girls and a boy. On the back is written: 'Petr with his grandchildren: Oz, Noa and Lihi. Ashkelon.'

I look at Ima and ask, 'Ima, who is Petr? And who are Oz, Noa and Lihi?'

'Petr Grinfeld is an adopted brother of Grandpa Gidi's. He lives in Ashkelon.'

'Interesting, now Grandpa Gidi suddenly has an adopted brother. Grinfeld, you said? That's the name written on the tattered suitcase Grandpa Gidi has!'

'Yes, Petr Grinfeld. He still calls himself by that name.'

'Who adopted Petr? How is he Grandpa Gidi's brother? Gosh, how many mysteries in this family!'

'Petr's story is a hard and complicated one. I'll tell you when I have the opportunity, not now. And, you know what? I have something very important to give you. Something that will help you write the paper.'

'What do you have to give me?'

'It's a surprise, but I need to look for it. You'll get it tomorrow, but now, go to sleep. Good night.'

3
Koppel and the Clarinet

The next day, after everyone is asleep, Ima comes to me. She holds her hands behind her back and says, 'Roni, come to me.'

What shining eyes Ima has. So green, with many sparkles of light.

'You found the surprise you promised me?'

'What do you think?'

'So where is it?'

'Behind my back.'

I turn towards her back, but she turns around and hides what she has there. Then she sits down and says, 'Come, child. First a huge hug.'

I hug Ima, and then she puts a cassette on the table.

'What's this?'

'Don't you see? It's a cassette.'

'A real surprise. A cassette. What's on it?'

'It has many stories on it that will help you write a real "roots" paper. But that doesn't mean you won't need to rummage, ask and listen to people who are connected to your roots.'

Everyone who knows me knows I don't have much patience. I need everything to happen right here and now. So I run to my room right away, bring my cassette player, put the cassette in, and from it comes... you won't believe it, Grandma Reiseleh's voice. I know it immediately. This voice makes me so excited. This is my great-grandmother. Suddenly I see sights and colours, smell smells that I thought I had forgotten. My eyes fill with tears. Who recorded her? When?

Ima hugs me. 'You know, Roni, when I was your age, and this was many years ago, I also had to write a "roots" paper. I wrote my paper on some of the branches of our family. I didn't write about Mittyu and Reiseleh, my grandparents, because the paper I wrote about one branch of the family turned out to be so inclusive that I didn't have time to write about the others. Grandpa Gidi's parents made sure to record their story, in the hope that I would go on with the work. But I didn't. Now you have an important job.'

I start the cassette again and listen. Ima sits next to me. It's quiet in the house, with only Grandma Reiseleh's pleasant, musical voice coming from the cassette. I see her blue eyes again before me, she tickles me and smiles a wide, loving smile...

> The time has come to tell the story. We're not so young anymore, and not so healthy either. We wavered: do we stay silent till the end, or tell? Grandpa Mittyu had an idea: we should record. We decided to do this so that you, our dear children, will have 'roots'. How does the Passover Haggadah say it? 'You shall tell it to your children'...

The cassette turns, and the ribbon winds on its spool. I don't understand the things Great-grandmother is saying at all. Maybe things will become clearer later.

> Koppel Scheiner was a young, handsome youth. He was a well-known clarinet player, and used to play at the Jewish weddings and feasts in the village of Bushtina. This is a village in Czechoslovakia, in the heart of the Carpathian Mountains, among thick forests. In one

of the weddings he played at he met a beautiful girl, Gita Shimshovitz, whom everyone called Gitale. He went on playing, but never took his eyes off her all that time. When he finished, he went over to her. His eyes blazed from excitement, and from that time...

I stop the cassette player. I don't understand what these names have to do with me. And who are these people?

'Ima, I think you're mistaken. The cassette talks about Koppel and Gitale. How are they connected to our family?'

'Roni, you're impatient. Listen for a few more moments, and you'll understand. You're closely connected to Koppel and Gitale.'

'But, Ima, what do these strange names mean?'

'Koppel is Yaakov. Gitale is Tova. In the Jewish village at Bushtina they called people by names close to the local language. Let's go on listening.'

I have to be more patient. Oh, all right...

The acquaintance between Koppel and Gitale deepened. They married, and had three children: Chaim, Dina, and me, Reiseleh. That's what my parents called me: Reiseleh. But in Hebrew, my name is Shoshana. I was the youngest and most mischievous in the family.

I know I'm impatient and want to know everything immediately, but I need to make some order: Koppel and Gitale are the parents of Great-grandmother Reiseleh, whose name is also Shoshana. Too bad she isn't alive anymore. I could sit opposite her, listen to the story from her own lips, and ask as many questions as I want. But she was really wise to have recorded herself. As though she knew she wouldn't be able to tell me when I grew up.

I go on listening.

Chaim, my brother, was a good boy – obedient, dedicated and industrious. Dina, my sister, who was older than I, was a beautiful, orderly girl. All her things were arranged in their places. The bed was always made, and all the books, notebooks and toys in their places. While I, the youngest, was always unruly, my clothes always unkempt. And … I would always run, jump and climb on everything that could be climbed. Ima and Abba were angry with me often, and sometimes would even spank me on the backside because I didn't agree to help put in order the mess I had made.

'Maybe you'll sit quietly for a bit,' Abba Koppel would scold me.

I remember Abba going out to his horses in the mornings, feeding them hay from the stable in the yard, getting on the wagon and setting off. Gitale, my mother, with the white coif on her head, worked all day. There was a water pump in the courtyard of our house. In the morning, even before we were up, Ima would already be in the courtyard, drawing water into huge containers and lugging them in. One for the shower, one for the kitchen… And already she would be standing, kneading dough, lighting the oven, putting potatoes on the fire, pickling salted fish, and by the time we got up the smell of buns had already spread all through the house. We quickly ate the bun, spread with butter Ima had churned from the milk she brought from the neighbours' cow shed. Ima Gitale made everything with her own hands, even the butter and cheeses, and we would run to school right after breakfast.

Ima had a heart of gold and hands of gold. She was always content with little, with her lot.

'You must pinch your cheeks before you go out,' Ima would say to Dina and me.

'Why?' I asked.

'Why? Because your cheeks must always be pink. So no one pities the Scheiner children. We don't need pity.'

And right after that she would entrust me with a pot filled with potato stew that she had already cooked that morning, to give to the orphan children who lived next door.

'What, they don't pinch their cheeks?' I asked Ima.

And truly, their cheeks weren't pink. They were poorly and pale.

My father, Abba Koppel, had a wagon hitched to two horses. He would drive the rich people from our village to the big city. We almost never saw Abba. He worked hard. He would leave the house in the morning before we woke up, and when he came back he would immediately put on his best clothes and go out to play his clarinet. He would come back from the parties he played at only after we all were fast asleep.

I remember I was once at our neighbour Miraleh's wedding. Ima sewed pretty sky-blue frocks for me and Dinchu [Dina].

'I chose cloth this colour so it matches your beautiful eyes,' she said, and sat down to sew. She sat by the sewing machine for three days. She marked the cloth with chalk, cut, sewed, pinned and fitted the frocks for us. Sometimes we would get stuck by the pins and move, and Ima would scold, 'Enough fidgeting!'

That night we all went to the wedding. The whole village was there. The bride was beautiful in her long white dress, embroidered with a sparkling white thread. She had many pink beads around her neck.

The women all looked festive with the fancy coifs on their heads. Ima wrapped her head with a flowery coif too. She wore the green frock she had sewn a year before, her 'frock for weddings', she called it. It was a long frock, made of shiny fabric, and had a lace collar decorated with a burgundy ribbon. Ima even added a row of light green beads to her coif.

She was charming at the wedding, and Chaim, already fifteen, was wearing a suit. My brother was the handsomest boy in all Bushtina. All the girls would whisper together when they saw him. He was tall and upright, his eyes were big and green, and his hair a shiny black. I was so proud of him.

Dinchu and I sat down and watched the dancers. Then we looked at Abba. He had forgotten himself in his music. The Hassidic melodies made everyone get up from their places, even the saddest of the guests. When he got excited, everyone's feet danced and stamped. The women surrounded the bride in a circle, and the men surrounded the groom. One circle, then another, went round and round, the men lifted their hands to heaven, closed their eyes and danced enthusiastically. The prayer shawl tassels flew round their waists, their cheeks were flushed, perspiration flowing down their faces and gathering in their collars. Many undid their neckties and stamped even faster, and Abba went on playing more and more strongly.

Dinchu and I got up from our places as well; even though we were shy, we simply couldn't go on sitting. I put my hands on Dinchu's waist and we both spun like a *dreidel* [a Jewish spinning top]. And suddenly, there was quiet. Abba stopped the melody for a moment, and everyone stood, breathless, wiping their faces. Even Abba took out the white wedding handkerchief Ima had sewn and embroidered, and wiped his face as well. He breathed deeply, took a drink of something, took up the clarinet and went on playing. Now he played a slow and calm melody. The dancers moved slowly, like waves, around the bride and groom, and then a long call of the clarinet and the rhythm got faster. Abba was ruling the steps of everyone here. By his will things happened. He wanted them to dance slowly, and they did it. He made them jump high if he wanted to. If he wanted them to surround the bride and groom in circles, they did it. And so, all night.

I stop the tape recorder and look at my mother. Her eyes shine.

4
Love at First Sight

I prepare the atlas to ask Grandpa some questions.

'Where is Karpathoros?' I ask Grandpa Gidi on the phone.

'Take out the atlas, Ronchu. I'll wait.'

'It's right here, Grandpa.'

'Page through and look for the map of Eastern Europe. Have you found it? Look for Czechoslovakia on the political map. Do you see it?'

Ima and I sit and look at the atlas. Here are the Carpathian Mountains in Czechoslovakia. The Ung River passes through them, and the Volga as well. I leaf through the postcards I found in the album. They have spectacular views. I see green boulevards of trees that drip with water, steeples of impressive churches, stylized buildings, bridges and canals, the streets filled with coffeehouses. I even 'hear' the music playing there. We have many recordings that Great-grandfather recorded, and we listen to them, especially on Shabbat [Sabbath].

We go back to the recording. Now Grandpa Mittyu's soft voice comes from the instrument. I try to see him before my eyes. His gentle, blue gaze cradles me in love. Ima sits by me too. She can't separate herself from these stories either. Ima's excitement blends with my own.

'I miss those two people so much,' Ima says, and wipes away a tear. We turn the cassette player back on. Grandpa Mittyu's voice comes out, melodiously.

> Grandma Reiseleh, my rose, grew up in a small village in Czechoslovakia, and I in the big city of Ungvar, on the Ung River. My father, Shmuel Grinfeld, owned a coffeehouse and a restaurant. We lived above the coffeehouse in a big and spacious house – I, my parents, my younger brother, Jutyu, and my younger sister, Helinka.
>
> We had a beautiful childhood. I was quite a boaster. I knew how to make acrobatic jumps into the river, and I did that especially when I wanted to impress the girls from the Hebrew gymnasium in Ungvar, when they stood on the banks. One time I made an exhibition jump high and wide into the water and... hit my head. I was able to float to the edge. My head was bleeding. I was able to get home, and there I had a 'reception' from Abba. Abba Shmuel was very stern. After bandaging my wound he gave me a strong slap across the face.
>
> 'How long will you act crazy? When will you be serious? When will you give some time to the violin?'
>
> Even now I miss that slap.
>
> We had a very unusual atmosphere at home. Ima and Abba worked hard at the coffeehouse, we studied, but when we came home we had to help, and I had to practise. Abba decided that I was the talented son of the family, like Mozart at the very least, and put much hope in me.

It sounds like Grandpa's voice cracked a little.

> Reiseleh, I'm going to make salad for supper. You go on telling for a while. I'll be right back...

Grandpa's voice sounds a bit distant.
Grandma Reiseleh starts speaking again.

> I loved spending time with friends. When I was sixteen I went with one of my good friends to one of the activities of the youth movement in the neighbourhood. I remember that I wore a blue frock that set off my eyes. The club for the 'Young Pioneer' movement was in Mittyu's house. The moment I entered the club he fixed his sea-blue eyes on me. I smiled back. From that moment I knew I would come to all the meetings.

I stop the cassette and close my eyes. I try to 'see' the happenings. I know Grandma Reiseleh had been a lovely girl. I had seen her in the photos. Upright, athletic, short hair, beautiful eyes. No wonder Grandpa Mittyu fell in love with her at first sight.

Grandpa had been a handsome boy as well. I look at the picture in the blue album. He is there in a tailored suit, with an impressive jacket and a necktie. Tall, broad-shouldered, and with a soft and dreamy gaze. This is exactly the gaze I remember. Even when he was old, he had the same gaze.

I press 'play', and hear Grandpa's voice again.

> Many young people from villages all over the whole district joined the 'Young Pioneer' movement. The movement had branches all over Czechoslovakia. Menachem Oren, our teacher from the gymnasium, came to the activities and told us about Israel. The things he said made a great impression on us. He spoke to us in Hebrew and excited us all. When he spoke we forgot the horrible war in Europe and the Germans coming closer and closer to Czechoslovakia. As I listened to him I looked at the new girl who had come to the club.
> She smiled at me.

5
Secrets I Must Find Out

When I come to Grandpa Gidi and Grandma Aliza's house I bring the cassette with me. I want to go on and listen together with the people who knew them well; Grandpa Gidi was Grandpa Mittyu and Grandma Reiseleh's own son.

Grandpa Gidi sits opposite me. He is dressed in his work clothes; a huge work frock that has seen better days. His hands are black from picking nuts. He sits and peels, peels and peels. He has a mountain of nuts by him. I try to help.

'No, Ronchu. This is my work. I don't want you to get your hands dirty. These black stains stay a long time. No cleaning fluid can get the pecan stains out.'

I stand behind him and fix his collar. I see a big scar on his neck.

'What's this scar, Grandpa? Since when do you have such a scar on your neck?'

'Roni, why are you asking so many questions? This isn't the time to ask about scars.'

'Grandpa, I've already asked you a few questions, and you always change the subject. You still haven't told me what the old dilapidated pacifier is doing in the brown suitcase. You've avoided telling me how the name "Grinfeld" is connected to you and your parents. Gosh, don't you understand that I'm not little Roni anymore? Don't you understand that I need your help to write the "roots" paper?'

'Just be a little patient...'

'Patience, patience. I'm really angry. How is it that you've still not told me about Petr Grinfeld? He's your adopted brother. I feel like you're always evading the issue. Why?'

'How did you hear about Petr Grinfeld?'

'From the picture in the album. I know he lives in Ashkelon, and I know he has grandchildren. I even have his phone number, and the email address for Noa, his granddaughter. I want to write to her.'

Grandpa looks at me in surprise.

'Roni, you're really quick. One day I'll tell you the story about Petr. Or, you know what? Maybe we should go to Ashkelon and you can hear the story right from the source. What do you think?'

'When will we go?'

'Slowly, Roni. Haste is from the devil.'

Again the 'slowly'...

With Grandpa Gidi, everything is always slow. He's so methodical, organized, doing everything comfortably. Exactly the opposite from Grandma Aliza. She's really frenetic. Everything is done quickly, and she does many things at once. Grandpa calls her 'the ventilator'.

Grandma comes over to me. She feels that I'm angry, and has made up a plate of surprises for me – peeled apple, sections of clementine, rings of banana and a few squares of chocolate.

'Eat, Roni, eat. Then we'll sit and listen to the cassette. You can ask me too. I'll tell you all I know.'

I'm still angry, in spite of Grandma's calming words. Why is Grandpa Gidi so evasive? He always finds an excuse to tell me as little as possible. What is he hiding? What is he ashamed of? Perhaps he is afraid? It would be interesting if my great-grandparents' story would solve the mystery of the pacifier, the scar and his adopted brother.

Now Grandma Aliza and I sit together and listen.

> When the 'Young Pioneers' meeting was over, we all sat and joked around together. Then, exactly what I wanted to happen actually happened. Mittyu came over to me, put out his hand and said, 'My name is Mittyu. I live here, above the club. My parents gave this room next to the coffeehouse and the restaurant my father manages, to the movement. My parents prefer to watch over me and my brother, Jutyu, from close by. Look, he's sitting opposite us. Will you come to the activity next week as well? I hope to see you.'
>
> I was so impatient for the next meeting. This time I asked my sister, Dina, to come as well. Ima and Abba were very angry.
>
> 'What do you and the Pioneers have in common? Stop this nonsense. There's so much work at home.'
>
> Abba is frowning. We argued a lot, but I won. I was very mischievous, and my parents had to give in. Dina still wavered, but Ima said to her: 'Go, Dinchu, go too, and watch over your mischievous sister.'
>
> Ima didn't trust me. She thought I needed a bodyguard... So we both went to the meeting at the club. Immediately I came in, Mittyu came over, smiling.
>
> 'I was waiting for you. I knew you would come. This is your sister, isn't it? You're similar,' he said.

A pause in the recording.

> From the moment I saw Reiseleh I had no rest. I thought about her all the time. I counted the days, the hours, the minutes between meetings. I thought about her all the time and everywhere. I didn't listen to the teachers in school, I only stared at them and thought of Reiseleh. Even when I was playing the violin I saw her before my eyes. I couldn't concentrate on anything except our next meeting. I didn't tell anyone about my plans. I need to clarify them with Reiseleh first.
>
> By the time a month had passed we had become quite good friends. I sat with Reiseleh in the kitchen at our house, holding her

hand, and said: 'Listen to me very closely. The Germans are getting close to Czechoslovakia. We cannot sit quietly. I want to leave here. I want to go to Eretz Israel.'

Reiseleh looked at me with her big eyes, and started crying.

'What happened? Why are you crying?'

'Don't you understand? My parents won't let me leave home. Don't you see that I always come to meetings with my sister, Dinchu? I'm lucky that she found a boyfriend here too, Yosef Adler. Mittyu, if you are going to Israel, the relationship between us will be over.'

'No, little one,' I answered her. 'I certainly am not going to let our relationship end. I want us all to get out of this hell. All of us. All your family and all of mine. I'm sure that whoever stays here will have a terrible time. Didn't you hear from Menachem, the leader, about what's happening in Poland? Didn't you hear about the horrors – the ghettos, the labour camps, the abuse, the new German laws? Don't you feel the hatred towards the Jews? The only place we can live as Jews is the land of Israel. You must understand.'

Reiseleh interrupts Mittyu.

When Dinchu and I came home, I asked her what she thought about *aliyah* to Israel. She looked at me in astonishment: 'Are you crazy? Do you really think Ima and Abba will allow it?'

'No, we will all make *aliyah*, with Ima, Abba and Chaim.'

'Now you're really dreaming. Don't you know what's waiting for you at home if you talk about these thoughts? Abba will be beside himself, Ima will be angry, her blood sugar will go up, she'll be more ill, and... Don't you dare tell. You and your big mouth. Watch it now, all right? If you talk they won't allow us to go to activities anymore, and then your relationship with Mittyu will be over, and mine with Yosef. Promise me you won't say a word.'

I didn't sleep all night. Hard thoughts passed through my head. *How do I tell my parents? Is this really the right way?*

6
Arguments and a Wedding

I've begun writing the paper. I summarize what I heard on the cassette. I've added a map of Czechoslovakia and a short account of what happened there during World War Two. I've read about the Jews from Karpathoros. Now I know that there were more than one hundred thousand Jews there before the war, but only 10,000 of them survived. They all died in Auschwitz and Treblinka.

I'm starting to understand a bit about the eulogy Grandpa Gidi read over Grandpa Mittyu's grave: 'Abba was right.' Things are slowly getting clearer, but I still have many questions. Now even Ima says to me: 'Slowly, Roni, slowly, patience.' But as you already know, I need to know everything at once. That's me – I have no patience.

Grandpa Gidi was very afraid when I wanted to throw away the old, dilapidated white pacifier. Why?

I go on listening to the recording. Now I hear Grandpa Mittyu's voice.

> We had many arguments at home. My parents decided to close the hall for the 'Young Pioneer' meetings. They thought we were being brainwashed. My parents were living in denial. They made a good living from their coffeehouse and received much respect from the people around them – even from their non-Jewish friends – and did not imagine that the situation was likely to change. They saw nothing else.

'We will immigrate to Israel even if you object,' Jutyu and I repeated to Ima and Abba.

'What do you have in common with that desert?' I saw Abba Shmuel's angry eyes. 'To leave such a beautiful country, full of forests and water, a good living, studies, violin, and go to pave roads in the desert? To make the desert blossom with heat and fever? Exchange a big and rich home for a tent in the desert? Who will give you a certificate to immigrate? Haven't you heard of the British Mandate's policy? Don't you know that the British rule there and don't allow anyone to immigrate? Enough, stop your nonsense. Enough with the arguments.'

Abba wiped his forehead, sat down in the armchair in the corner of the room, and listened to music to calm himself, as was his custom.

This is the moment for a short pause, in order to clarify some things.

'Grandpa, tell me about the Mandate period and the whole certificate subject.'

Grandpa Gidi smiles. 'It's lucky you have the "punishment" of writing a 'roots' paper. The certificate is a licence, permission to make *aliyah* to Israel. When the British ruled here they didn't allow Jews to immigrate, because they didn't want to annoy the Arabs in Israel. The Arabs, who felt that they were the owners of the land, wanted it for themselves, and feared that if many Jews immigrated they would become a minority.'

'But the land of Israel is our land, the land of the Jews, isn't it?'

'Yes, Roni. But the Arabs in Israel weren't willing to hear of a Jewish state being founded here.'

'And what is a mandate?' Not that I don't know, but I want Grandpa to tell me.

'A mandate is a power of attorney to govern a certain place. The League of Nations gave Britain the mandate to govern the land of Israel."

'Who are the League of Nations?'

Wow, so many things I need to learn in order to understand my great-grandparents' story. How can I understand things if there are so many words I don't know?

I go back to the cassette. Grandpa Mittyu goes on:

So I answered my father that I knew everything. I know about the hardships connected with receiving an entry permit. I know that many of the Jews make *aliyah* even without the permission, by *ha'apala* – illegal immigration. I also know that the voyage to Israel is in crowded freight ships. But in spite of everything I remain committed to my desire to make aliyah.

'I'm already grown, Abba. I think it's right that Jutyu and I make *aliyah*, and work the land. You, Ima and Helinka can follow us.'

Abba was so angry he was beside himself. His face grew red, and he was shaking. Ima came to help. She brought him a glass of cold water and turned to Jutyu and me.

'Enough with the arguments! Ever since you started this there's been no peace in this house. Mittyu, don't you see what you're doing? Enough. I don't want to hear another word about Israel. Our home is here in Czechoslovakia. Our living is here. Your studies are here also. And that's it.'

Ima burst into tears. Deep inside I knew she agreed with us, but...

Abba sat in his armchair. His face still flamed. It was hard for him to calm down. In spite of the fact that he was so angry, I didn't stop myself. I felt I had to say things as they were. I sat down next to him and went on speaking quietly, logically.

'Abba, I prefer paving roads there, in Israel, in the desert, in the heat and the dust, to living here in fear. And maybe not living at all.'

Abba opened his eyes wide and sent me a piercing glance. I saw all the sorrow of the world in those eyes. That glance haunts me to this day. I'm sure Abba understood, but he preferred to remain silent.

I left the room quietly. I learned that our bold ideas must be 'dripped' in, drop by drop. I went up to my room and sat down to write to Reiseleh. She hadn't come to the meetings for two weeks now. Now, with the club in our home closed, I don't know when I'll see her again. I miss her so much.

Again a pause in the cassette. Grandpa Mittyu gives his place to Grandma.

I received a very long letter from Mittyu. Many of the letters were blurred, perhaps from tears. I had a small brown suitcase where I hid all my secrets. I pushed it far under my bed, but I'm not sure my mother didn't peek inside. She knew much more than I ever told her. Today I forgive her for it. I know she was worried and wanted to know what was happening to her mischievous daughter.

I hid the letter I received from Mittyu in the little suitcase. When no one was in the room, I sat and wrote him a letter in return. I wrote about how I missed him, about my parents, who didn't allow Dinchu and me to leave the house, and how sad I was. I went to school, but I couldn't concentrate. My head was full of thoughts, and the chief of them was when I could see Mittyu again.

Dinchu barely heard what anyone said to her, and she missed her wise and shrewd Yosef. She too received letters from him. We would both sit in our room at night, after Abba, Ima and Chaim had fallen asleep, light the lamp and read the letters over and over again. We would read and write into the small hours of the night.

We found out that not far away was another branch of the 'Young Pioneers'. We went there and met many other young people. Everyone was stirred up about everything that was happening. The Germans were already at the gates of Czechoslovakia. They were conquering at the speed of the wind, exiling, destroying, burning everything belonging to Jews. We heard, too, of their abuse toward other minorities, gypsies, ill people, mentally challenged people, dwarves, whoever they didn't like. I was only seventeen then, but I had already decided: I am not going to stay and live here. *I must leave for Israel.*

And my parents? *I will try to convince them. I will also try to persuade Chaim, my brother. He has completely lost his head. He has a girlfriend, and they are already talking about marriage.* Abba promised to play at their wedding, to give them the most joyful wedding around. Ima promised to sew Sheindele's wedding dress. *I know what is waiting for me at home. They will probably say that I'm only seeing my own side, that I don't care about Ima who is ill and Abba who works so hard, that I am a mischievous sparrow, flying wherever she wants, with no thought for the family.*

My parents were busy now preparing for Chaim's wedding with Sheindele Hermann. They loved Sheindele from the first moment.

'You look like Reiseleh. You have the same eyes and the same smile,' they said to her repeatedly. This was enough to indicate that they saw her as a daughter.

Ima stood in the kitchen for many hours. Women from the neighbourhood came to help with the preparations, and together they baked cakes, *challahs*, *kiplach* biscuits and *rugelach*, they cooked jam, pickled vegetables – cabbage, carrots and turnips – and fish. What a commotion. In the confusion it was easy for Dinchu and me to escape to branch meetings of the movement. They were speaking there about what was happening all around.

My parents didn't have the strength to fight us anymore. They understood that our desire to be part of this strange group of 'Young Pioneers' was stronger than they were. The winds of war were blowing strongly. Menachem, the teacher we met at the club when it was at Mittyu's house, came himself one day. He spoke about the Zionist work in Israel, told us about the hardships we were likely to meet with there, but planted in us much confidence in our own strength and abilities. He taught us what cooperation was, and told us about the *hachsharah*, the agricultural training in Prague.

'When you get to Prague, they will train you to be ready to make *aliyah* to the Land. You'll learn how to work in agriculture, in construction, and in paving roads. They will teach you how to fight the laws of the Mandate, take care of your illegal immigration papers and give you passports,' he said.

When we came back home we got the amount of anger that was due to our amount of rebellion.

'What are you doing? Instead of helping to prepare for your brother's wedding, you're busy with nonsense?'

Chaim was married two weeks later. What a special wedding it was. The joy reached the heavens. Abba made everyone dance, and we danced till the morning light. There was no one more joyful than Chaim, our brother, and his wife shone with gladness as well. She looked like an angel in her white dress that suited her slender body so well. She danced with utter abandon, and the women who surrounded her clapped, and then carried her on their shoulders. Such joy!

7
Farewell

Reiseleh continues:

Now more than ever we were hearing about the catastrophe befalling the Jews in countries conquered by the Germans. Our parents were aware of the Germans' appetite to conquer the whole world, and Czechoslovakia as well. Abba now understood that we were justified in going to the *hachsharah* in Prague. He no longer protested when we told him about the 'Young Pioneers' meetings. Ima even cooperated with us, but she was very sad. She was ill. Her blood sugar had gone up very much, and she needed Dinchu's and my help. She still smiled at us, and her smile filled our hearts with love for her. Ima had packed our suitcases. I had an orange suitcase, and Dinchu a bigger brown one. They were clearly labelled with our names. We packed them with all our secrets and letters.

Chaim and Sheindele, his wife, had come. Sheindele was pregnant. They asked that we send them information about the *hachsharah* in Prague, and if possible about the illegal immigration as well. Perhaps they would join us later. Chaim crushed me in his embrace.

'Reiseleh, little sister, watch over yourself, do you hear? And send letters. We'll see each other soon.'

Before we left the house, Ima went into the kitchen. She gave us the colourful biscuit tin, packed with biscuits for the journey, especially the sugared *kiplach* biscuits that we love so much.

We stood wrapped in her embrace for a long time. I heard her heartbeat and felt her tears fall on my hair. She didn't get into Abba's wagon with us. She stood, sad, waving her emaciated hand and choking down her tears.

Abba sat, quiet, sunk in his own thoughts. He spurred the horses on and the wagon moved quickly. Abba took out a handkerchief and wiped his eyes. Abba, the stern man who internalized everything, wiped the tears from his cheeks and from his beard that recently became white. Our hearts ached.

When would I see Ima again? The doctor had made it clear that she must inject herself with insulin every day. I was the one who would go to the chemist and buy the medicine for her. Who would do it now? *Chaim and Sheindele are expecting a baby. Chaim most probably won't have time, and Abba works from morning till night.* Pangs of conscience assailed me. *I and my dreams. I've only been seeing myself in all this. And Dinchu, she sits and cries. I know it's especially hard for her. She is the good girl who is so close to our parents and who always helps at home – she is the one who is leaving.*

Abba broke the silence. 'I don't know what to say to you, dear girls,' he began. 'I don't know if you're doing the right thing. But I'm not stopping you. Each day is getting harder. Maybe this really is the time to set out...'

When we arrived at the train station, Abba tied the horses and went down with us onto the platform. He looked so tired and old. His shoulders were bowed and his face was filled with wrinkles.

The train arrived. We hugged Abba and he embraced us with his strong arms.

'Write. Tell us what happens. Perhaps we will join you as well. If only the cursed Germans keep away from our town long enough.'

The parting from Abba was a tearful one. We got into the train carriage. The train began to move. Abba ran after it, waving a white handkerchief. I continued watching the man running after the train. His image became smaller and smaller, till it disappeared completely.

8
A Letter

Again I page through the album. It's as if the people speaking in the cassette wake into life. I look at a small photo: Reiseleh is standing beside Dina and Chaim, and behind them is their mother. A coif covers her head, and beside her is her husband, Koppel, wearing strange clothes; wide trousers and a white shirt, and over it a sort of black coat. His beard is meticulously combed. Grandfather Koppel had been a handsome man.

I rummage through the suitcase, and find a letter written in a feminine hand. How can I read the small, faded letters? Who can help me?

When Ima returns from work, even before she puts down her bag, I pounce on her with questions: 'Do you know who wrote this letter? Do you think what's written here can be deciphered?'

Ima sits down and looks through the pages and letters I have found in the suitcase. She tries to put them in some kind of order. The script in most of the letters is faded. Ima takes the letters where the script is relatively clear, and puts them in a big envelope.

'I'll take the letters to our photographer. He knows how to reconstruct documents. Perhaps he will be able to photograph the letters so that the script will be clearer.'

'Who will be able to read us the letters written in this foreign language?'

'You're being impatient again. Don't you trust me?'

The next day, when Ima returns from work she is holding a big brown envelope. I know that these were the letters. She takes five photographed pages out of the envelope; the script on them is fairly clear.

'Come on, Ima, how will we know what is written here?'

'On Shabbat we will visit Uncle Yosef, the husband of Dinchu, may her memory be a blessing. Yosef is happy to welcome any acquaintance who visits him. He is very old, but he will surely be happy to read us the letters.'

I wait impatiently for Shabbat.

We are sitting now in Uncle Yosef's house in Ramat HaSharon. He smiles at me and says: 'You know, Roni, you inherited your beautiful blue eyes from Grandmother Reiseleh. Exactly the same eyes.'

'Uncle Yosef, can you decipher what is written here in the letters?'

I give him a letter dated 22 February 1939.

'This is a letter written many years ago, before I was born,' says Grandma Aliza.

'And over a year before I was born,' says Grandpa Gidi.

Yosef laughs. 'And I was almost twenty. Mittyu was about my age.'

Yosef puts on his spectacles, smooths the paper with his hand, coughs, and wipes his nose with a big handkerchief.

'Wait a moment; maybe we should drink something first,' he says, and goes to the kitchen.

He quickly returns with a tea tray. He has prepared a cup of milk for me. Yosef thinks I'm still a baby.

When we are finished drinking, Yosef clears his throat, puts on his spectacles again, smooths the paper once more, and begins to read:

My dear Reiseleh,
   I'm sending this letter to you with Menachem.
   Reiseleh, you cannot imagine how I miss you. I wait impatiently for the moment when we will meet again.
   There are arguments at our house day and night. We haven't been studying at our Hebrew gymnasium for weeks now. We all speak excitedly about happenings in Europe, about the war and about the rumours from the conquered countries. The rumours say that in nearby Poland all the Jews have been gathered into ghettos. Can you imagine, Reiseleh, four families crammed in one apartment? By order of the Gestapo the Jews have built a wall five metres high around the ghetto. No one can escape. The Nazis have stolen the Jews' spacious homes and given them to Polish families. This is injustice personified: a cramped apartment for four families, in exchange for the spacious houses the Jews were forced to give up.
   The Germans take strong Jewish boys for forced labour for their war effort. They take advantage of all the strength of youth. Whoever doesn't withstand the harsh conditions simply dies. We hear hair-raising rumours of corpses piled up and buried in holes. Other forced labourers arrive in trains to take the place of those who did not survive. The trains run on their tracks day and night. More and more Jews are taken to the camps.
   We speak much of the *hachsharah* in Prague. The way is shorter from there to the illegal immigration routes. Menachem, our guide and teacher, has convinced us that this is the way. When I come home I try to help Abba. There is much work in the coffeehouse, serving, clearing, cleaning, even baking cakes. I tried to help Ima also, but she is so angry all the time because I want to go to the *hachsharah* that she doesn't talk to me about the subject.
   Her eyes are swollen from crying. Apparently she cries all night. But I'm sure she understands us. When she is alone with Abba she must be trying to convince him. She still doesn't speak with me about it. She wants peace at home. It is clear to me that one wrong word and there will be another earthquake. I love Ima and admire her worry for us all, but we, Jutyu and I, make her angry with our plans.

Our Helinka also wants to join us, but she is too young. She is only fifteen.

This is very hard for me. Because of the fear of the unknown, but also because of the war, because of the information about what is happening to the Jews, but especially because of Ima, Abba and Helinka. It is hard for us to leave them here. Our suitcases are already packed. Lately Abba looks more sad than angry. Apparently he understands that we should all leave.

Reiseleh, I'll stop here and write more in a few days.

• • •

Jutyu and I have finished packing. This is it. We are ready to leave for the train station. Tomorrow we will already be in Prague. You won't believe it, Reiseleh. Abba came over to me, hugged me and said: 'Mittyu, you have always been rebellious. You always dragged Jutyu after you. I've been thinking a lot about what has happened. You could be right. Time will tell.' He took a small prayer book off the shelf, gave it to me, and said, full of emotion: 'I can't help you anymore, so may the Holy One, Blessed be His Name, be your help,' and my strong father burst into tears.

Ima came over to us. She held a parcel in her hand, tied with string.

'Take it. It is provisions for the journey. I've made you some of the *kiplach* you love. Take care of yourselves. And this,' she said and gave me a small box, 'this is a ring my mother gave me. I hoped to give it to your wife, Mittyu, when the time came. Take it with you. For you, Jutyu, I have a diamond necklace. Perhaps you will need it...'

We went with Ima and Abba to the train station. I still feel Ima's salty tears that wet my cheek when she kissed me, and still see before my eyes my big, strong Abba, weeping bitterly. Even the *kiplach* Ima packed for us tastes of tears. Helinka, my sister, wept also and hugged me so hard. She thought she could stop me that way.

I miss them so much, and miss you too, my Reiseleh.

I embrace you with all my strength. When will we meet?

Love, Mittyu.

Yosef lifts his eyes from the page. This letter, written in Hungarian, has taken him back to his home in Karpathoros, to his family murdered in Auschwitz, and to Dinchu, his wife, who died about ten years ago. I promise that next time I see him I will bring *kiplach*. I understand that these biscuits taste of his home in Czechoslovakia.

I thank Yosef and promise to come again.

'You won't get rid of me so easily,' I say.

Yosef smiles at me and his eyes, full of goodness, touch my heart.

'I'll be waiting for you.'

9
Fear and Joy

It's already evening. I'm so tired. I'll be going to bed in a minute. Suddenly the door opens. My father is here at last. I haven't seen him for a few days now. He is working around the clock. I'm happy that this evening I'll be able to exchange a few words with him. My brother and sisters are already asleep.

'Abba,' I say to him right after the hug, 'I don't understand how Reiseleh and Mittyu had the courage to get up and leave home when they were so young. I don't know if I could do what they did. Abba, do you think that you would have rebelled against your parents and left, even if you knew you might never see them again?'

'It's hard to judge. Times were different then. It was a very hard war that went on for six years. A war that many countries participated in. They didn't call it a world war for nothing! It was much harder than World War One. The Germans had a detailed plan to wipe out all of European Jewry. They called it the "Final Solution". They wanted to "clean" the world of Jews, and felt superior to anyone who didn't have Aryan blood in their veins. They thought they were the master race – the Aryan race – and believed that different, better blood flowed through their veins than what flowed through the veins of the rest of humanity.

'The propaganda was very persuasive. The Jews were presented as monsters, fleas, rats, as lice that needed to be got rid of. Whole crowds of people were influenced by the propaganda. They believed the lies that were heaped on the Jews. Hitler promised those who supported him a living, a big place to live in, and took care to convince his people that the economic situation in Germany was bad because of the Jews. Many people were sure that the "Final Solution" would save them, and that they would be able to make a living and have large houses.'

'Abba, how could they even think that they would be saved by the destruction of another people? I don't get it.'

I sit talking with Abba for a long time. I try to understand what has happened. I go to sleep confused. Tomorrow after school I must sit with the cassette and listen. Maybe I will find answers there for all the questions running through my head.

Morning arrives and the sun is already warming the air. I get up for a new day. Ima has already made us breakfast. Today I have a lot to do. Right after I come back from school and finish the annoying homework that the teachers give us, I'll sit and listen.

Everything goes according to plan. Now I am free, and go on listening. Reiseleh's voice rings out:

We came to the *hachsharah* camp in Prague. It consisted merely of three tumbledown houses. The girls lived in one house, the boys in another, and the third was for storing work tools, food and other items.

I worked in the cemetery from morning till night. I weeded, cleaned, planted and pruned. I was a good, industrious worker. The money we earned was intended for the whole group. We needed to prepare for the illegal immigration: get *aliyah* permits, food and medicine, find ships and get them refitted, and all this would cost much money. In the evening we would meet and learn about the history of the land of Israel, and hear reports of what was happening there. We were waiting for the day when we would receive the permission for *aliyah*.

Our organizing institutions made every effort to get as many exit permits for the Land as possible. The British didn't want to give any permits above the quota limit. The Jewish Agency, which was meant to receive these permits, preferred to give them to the young adults, the youth and the children. The older ones among us could wait. I thought of my parents. They would of course not be given a permit so quickly. They were too old, and Ima was ill.

We had preferential treatment here as well. I didn't know any more what was right and good. I thought that especially the old people should be given an escape. The young had more strength to survive and escape the evil that would come. My friends thought differently. They thought that the children hadn't been able to do anything yet, and all their lives were before them. So many thoughts... In the meantime, we were still working and waiting.

I hadn't seen Mittyu. Apparently he and his brother had been sent somewhere else.

One evening one of the guides asked to see us all. He has important things to tell everyone at camp, he said.

And indeed, he announced with a stern face: 'I hope we won't be forced to stay here for much longer. The situation in Europe is worsening from day to day. The Jews are in danger everywhere. New limitations are put on us, and here at camp the rules have changed as well. From today we must return to camp by six in the evening, and it is forbidden for us to stay outside. Whoever does not obey is likely to pay for it with their lives. You may not have heard, but the Germans are already right on the outskirts of Czechoslovakia.'

I was filled with worry. What would happen to my parents, my brother and his wife? What would happen to the Jews in my town?

The guide took yellow cloths out of a big bag, and gave one to each of us. He called it a 'yellow patch', and it had a Star of David on it.

'You must wear this patch when you leave camp.'

'Why?' we all asked as one.

'So that whoever sees you will know you are Jewish. Whoever

doesn't wear it and is found to be Jewish endangers himself and the others as well.'

In spite of the boundless anger, we decided that it was better not to resist the Germans who instituted these laws. We all wore the 'yellow patch'.

I remember that one day, as I was on my way to work, someone spit on me. For no reason at all, he just passed by me and spat in my face. Truly a great hero! It was a testimony of how far the hate had come. What had I done to him? I went on walking as though nothing had happened, but that humiliation burns within me to this day. I was afraid to go out without the patch, and I was ashamed to go out with the patch. Every action had to be surveyed carefully, from every direction. Anti-Semitism was rearing its head everywhere.

One day I was walking in the street, and I covered the patch with my hand. A Czech Gentile [non-Jew] coming from the opposite direction pushed my hand aside, gave me a resounding slap across the face and said: 'Don't cover the patch, little Jew. Everyone can see it.'

We suffered very much from the anti-Semitism of the Czechs. Many of them cooperated with the Germans. I don't know if they did it out of fear, or because of being brainwashed. Perhaps they too thought they would receive a house and a job if they cooperated? The confiscation of Jewish property had already begun: houses, works of art, cars, electric appliances and even coats. Everything 'for the war', 'for the Reich'. Rumours passed among us about German soldiers going into houses and taking whatever they wanted.

I was so worried for my family.

About a week after the incident with the Gentile I was riding a streetcar on the way to work. Opposite me sat a Jew wearing a grey suit, a white shirt, a blue tie, a beautiful hat on his head, a white, dignified beard on his face and a patch on his sleeve. Czech young men came over to him, laughing, and kicked him, slapped him across the face and spat on him. The Jew begged for his life, and tried to protect his head with his hands from the blows landing on him. I saw the whole thing, but didn't rise from my seat. I was left paralyzed. What could I have done?

The streetcar raced ahead, and the young men dragged the Jew from his place, took his hands and feet and threw him out as though he had been a sack of potatoes.

I came back to camp afraid, ashamed and humiliated. What would happen? Would we be able to leave in time? What about my family? Suddenly... I couldn't believe my eyes. Mittyu was walking towards me. My eyes filled with tears. He was so changed. His face was so thin. He no longer had the same pink cheeks or the same light in his eyes. I ran to him. I clung to him. We stood for a long time in each other's arms, and I felt my tiredness and humiliation melt away. His arms around me and his heartbeat against mine gave me new life. I felt secure and protected.

'What happened, little girl? What are these tears? Enough, enough.'

I told him everything. My whole body trembled and Mittyu soothed: 'Shh... Shh... We will get to Israel. Everything will be good, you'll see.'

10
The Covenant

I am now summarizing the Nuremberg Laws, and I can't believe that human beings thought them up. How does one kill a people legally? Wasn't law meant to defend humanity? There, in Nuremberg, laws were written that were intended to kill a whole people. Because a Jew is not a citizen of the Reich, he has no rights nor legal defence. His life and possessions are legally forfeit.

I am angry. The descriptions I've read have shocked me. Gathering the Jews into horribly crowded ghettos, fencing them in behind high walls, prey to evil-hearted people who abuse them and throw them from a moving train? Marking Jews as though they were cattle…

Abba and Ima feel that I am sad, but they do not have an answer for the many questions I ask, even though they want very much to comfort me.

'Roni,' Ima looks at me with her eyes that are full of goodness, 'it's hard to explain what happened. Hitler was a complete madman.'

Abba hugs me: 'These things happened long ago. It's important that we should remember them. It's important that we tell our children, our grandchildren and great-grandchildren everything. We must not forget what happened to the Jewish people; these things must not happen again. We must always look at what is happening, and stop bad waves before they break, and destroy an entire world in their path.'

'But why the Jews? Why?'

'I don't understand it either. No answer can explain why these things happened. I know the Gentiles were jealous of the Jews. In Germany and in other European countries there were many Jews who were honoured, scholarly, wealthy holders of high professions. The Jews' wealth caused envy.'

'What, no one should be rich? No one should be scholarly and of good standing? No one should have a good job? And if the Jews had been poor, the Holocaust wouldn't have happened? Why did the Germans persecute the gypsies? Were they jealous of them too? Why did they persecute dwarves, and ill and physically impaired people?'

I sit for a long time with my parents. The more I ask, the more I see that they have fewer and fewer answers.

I go back to the cassette. Now I'm with Grandpa Mittyu.

> Next day we gave our details to the contact person in the camp in Prague. He was meant to go to the relevant offices to issue passports. The quota is so small. I hope we get the permission to immigrate to Israel.
>
> We try to live a normal life here. Dinchu has married Yosef in the meantime. Other couples have also married here, without a rabbi, without a Jewish ceremony, without a ring. We must go on, must raise families. We must overcome everything.
>
> It was late in the evening, and it was chilly outside. Reiseleh and I went walking on some of the paths around the camp, wearing our coats with the conspicuous yellow armbands. Waiting for the passports shredded our nerves. I wanted to make the girl by my side happy. She was so sad. I must protect her. I hugged her warmly and said: 'Reiseleh, I want to ask you to be my wife. You know how dear you are to me. I want to raise a family with you. I'm sure our lives will be better when we get to Israel. I dream about it at night. We'll

build a house there, maybe join a kibbutz. We'll have a little house and a little garden, flowers, mischievous children, lots of light. The sun will shine...'

Reiseleh clung to me. Her whole body shook. Was it cold? Fear? Or perhaps excitement?

'Reiseleh, I would like to ask that from this moment your name will be Shoshana. You will be my *shoshana,* my beautiful and fragrant rose. I'm called now by a Hebrew name as well. Not Mittyu anymore, but Moshe. Like Moses brought the people of Israel out of Egypt, I'll bring you out from here. What do you say?'

Reiseleh looked at me and smiled: 'What do you think – could I refuse such a proposal?'

She put her arms around my neck and gave me such a kiss that I can taste it even to this day.

We were married without music, without dancing and even without a rabbi. I took the ring Ima had given me before leaving out of my pocket. Ima had had just enough time to tell me: 'Mittyu, give this ring to the woman who will be your wife. This ring will remind you of me.' I put it on my Shoshana's finger, embraced her and vowed: 'I will build you a home, plant a tree, and together we will plant flowers. It will be good for us.'

We made a covenant with each other, and from that day we were husband and wife.

11
In the Transit Camp

We continued working. I [Reiseleh] tended the Christian cemetery, and Mittyu was a porter. He carried electric equipment on his back that the Germans had taken from Jews sent for 'resettlement'. He loaded all these possessions on lorries before they continued on. We didn't understand then. Everything was unclear. We knew that many of the Jews had packed and left. Where? We didn't really know. There were many contradictory rumours. Truthfully? In our heart of hearts we preferred not to know.

One morning I received a letter. I looked at the postmark, incredulous. The letter was from Bushtina, my own town. It was Abba's hand on the envelope. I opened it with trembling hands. My eyes filled with tears and the words became unclear. I took a deep breath, wiped my eyes and began reading.

Dinchu and Reiseleh, our dear daughters,

Congratulations. You are aunts. Chaim and Sheindele have a beautiful daughter. She is plump, soft and loves to smile. The little one has made me a grandfather, and your mother is Grandma Gitale. Chaim and Sheindele have not yet decided on a name. We spend a lot of time with the baby. Ima does not stop smiling. She holds the baby and melts from the touch. She has such a good smell too! She has brought light to us all. Rita, Sheindele's sister, has come here from London. She wasn't able to withstand the temptation, and has come to see her first niece. She will spend only a short time here, but has already brought a breath of fresh air with her. She is young, beautiful – and stubborn.

When we saw her the first time, she took our breath away. She looks so like you, Reiseleh. Her husband has stayed in London. He is about to join the army.

Rita has brought many gifts for us all, and especially soft muslin frocks for the baby. She speaks much of London, and would even like us all to live there. 'There is a different life outside your village,' she says. We are trying to do everything to get permission for us all to immigrate to Israel, but we aren't cancelling London out either... The situation here is extremely bad. Many young men have been taken from the villages for the war effort. I hope that our Chaim will not be taken. All I ask of you, please, is that you take care of yourselves.

We all miss you, and feel your absence very much.

Warm kisses from us all. We love you, and believe that your decision was right and just.

A big hug from us, Ima and Abba

Mittyu came in then. He took hold of my trembling shoulders. When he read the letter, he was very moved. We went into our room and began writing letters. Dinchu and I wrote to Ima and Abba, to Chaim, Sheindele and the baby in Bushtina, and Mittyu and Jutyu wrote to their home in Ungvar. We hoped the letters would arrive. We prayed that we would have the privilege of seeing our family in Eretz Israel.

Many months had gone by, and we still had no answers about the passports. Letters from home hadn't arrived either. The atmosphere outside the camp was very hard. No Jew could be seen in the streets. Everyone was hiding in their houses. Many had vanished. Everything was vague.

Dinchu had given birth, fortunately to a strong, healthy boy. He was called Yitzhak, after Yosef's father. Dina and Yosef called him Yitzhakleh. He filled all our hearts with joy. Light was beginning to break through the darkness. Yosef was happy. He couldn't stop visiting our shack and followed his Yitzhakleh's every move. I was increasing in size too! Soon I would give birth as well. I hoped the child that was born would live in a free world, not in the horrible fear that paralyzed us all.

Not long before this, we were moved away from Prague to a different transit camp in Bratislava, the city on the Danube. We were lodging in an ugly and horrible 'hotel' called *Slovodarna*. If the passport we were so eagerly waiting for arrived, it would be easier to sail from there to a port on the Black Sea, and from there to take a ship to Eretz Israel.

I had packed again, and condensed all my belongings into one suitcase. I made some order in the small brown suitcase, put all the letters and pictures from home into a tin, and put the blue album I brought from home on the bottom. I crammed rags made of sheets into the corners. They would be nappies for the baby when he was born.

The hotel was dingy, but the city was glorious. It had many church towers and impressive buildings, and the river flowed through it.

Grandpa goes on telling:

This hotel was a concentration camp in all but name, where young people from all the Nazi-conquered countries – Austria, Czechoslovakia and Germany – lived in shameful conditions. The managers of this hotel were Fascist Slovaks who collaborated with the Germans, and some SS officers as well. They 'took care' to humiliate and abuse us at every turn. Their hatred for the Jews knew no bounds.

The hotel consisted of many long, narrow shacks that had been meant for storing grain. There were gaps in the wooden planks that surrounded the shacks. This hotel had no doors either. We shut ourselves in using tin panels, wood, anything we could find. The wind came in and chilled us to our bones. We comforted ourselves with the thought that our suffering was temporary.

In spite of the hard work we were tasked with in the upkeep of the hotel, we did our best to live a normal life. Everybody helped everybody. We had dentists present, a GP, craftsmen – a shoemaker, a carpenter and a bricklayer – and teachers for nursery and primary school as well. When these were free of their regular work they would gather the children, tell them stories, teach them songs in Hebrew, and each one would do his part to help his friends keep as normal a life as possible.

More people arrived at the hotel daily. Some among them were refugees who had escaped the convoys to the extermination camps, and two who had even escaped the extermination camp itself. Repeatedly they told us what had happened to them. We heard of pogroms, hard labour in forced labour camps, starvation, and worst of all – the wholesale destruction meant to purge Europe of Jews; for the first time we heard of crematoriums. 'The Germans are galloping ahead and annexing increasing amounts of land from the European countries. They have already conquered part of Romania,' said one of the refugees.

He stood among us, emaciated and frightened, skin and bones. I thought to myself: if we do get an exit permit, we'll need to get to a port in Romania. I tried to make myself forget this new trouble, in the hope that we would be able to get through this as well.

The refugee went on to tell that countries that were conquered and annexed to the Third Reich had begun collaborating with the Germans. The Germans are recruiting people from these countries to help them solve the 'problem'. Among other things, they recruited Jews of high standing in the community to act as 'liaisons'. These last were called 'Judenrat'. They were instructed to submit lists of Jews to be taken out of the ghetto for 'resettlement'. And woe to any of these Judenrat members who did not act as instructed. We all understood what 'resettlement' meant.

'I've heard of two from the Judenrat who have committed suicide,' the refugee told us. 'These cursed Germans are using us Jews to solve the "problem" quickly and efficiently.'

Here too in *Slovodarna* the rule was stern and stiff. We were abused, and our lives, hard in any case, were intentionally made harder. The hotel managers defined us as 'seasonal workers', and the overseers took as much advantage of us as they could. Most of them were perpetually drunk, and in their drunkenness abused us ceaselessly.

A long pause. Sighs came from the cassette. It's hard for Grandma Reiseleh to go back to that place...

I, with my huge belly, was forced to work in the kitchens and wash the cooking boilers. They were big, and I had to slide half my body inside them, even with my big belly, to wash the bottoms. I felt the baby inside me being pushed and crushed.

There was one officer there who must have liked me, in spite of my belly. He sent meaningful looks my way, and whenever I smiled at him in return he would lighten my workload a little. If I didn't he would give me unbearably hard work.

I wanted to go back to the camp in Prague so much. I missed the life there, even with all the hardship and humiliation I suffered. Mittyu never stopped encouraging me: 'Soon. A few days more and we'll be on our way to Israel.' I didn't believe it would happen. The passport seemed further away than ever.

12
Birth

My labour pains came late at night. I was confused. What should I do? I didn't want to wake my sister. She was asleep, with her baby beside her. I got up from my narrow bed quietly. The darkness outside was thick and quiet. Suddenly I heard a dog barking. I froze on the spot. When the quiet returned I went on, haltingly. The pains became stronger and stronger, and the barking with them. I got to the men's shack. I knocked on the tin door and someone opened it very slightly. I whispered to him: 'Call Mittyu, quickly please.'

Mittyu was there in seconds. He was agitated and confused. When he came to his senses he took his faded coat, and put it around my shoulders. The camp guard was sleepy. It was doubtful if he understood what was happening. I tried to explain but he didn't seem to want very much detail. He opened the gate, and we both went out.

We came to the main street. A streetcar stopped next to us; luckily there were no passengers. Bad things could have happened there, and no one would have known a thing. We trembled from cold and fear, and I from pain as well. The labour pains were very strong.

We got off at the last station and walked on foot to the hospital. Mittyu supported me, and I groaned quietly. The yellow patch shone on our sleeves, and we didn't dare stop any vehicles. The walk went on forever. The pains grew stronger. Mittyu encouraged me.

'Soon, Shoshana. A few more minutes. Breathe deeply. Yes, like that.' He breathed in and out, trying to make me laugh.

We came to the hospital. The maternity ward was full of people. A stern nurse put me in a side bed in the hall. The midwife came. Immediately she saw the yellow patch, and in a cold, decisive voice said to Mittyu: 'Out!'

I was in her hands. The pains were intolerable, but I swallowed the groans. Fear paralyzed me. She pressed my belly hard. Her pressing hurt more than the birth pains. She pressed aggressively, like someone who wanted to cause pain. I didn't know how far along I was in the birth. The midwife pressed again, and I didn't say a word. At last I began to cry. Just one kind word, and it would have been easier.

My tears made no impression on the midwife. Indeed, she pressed more strongly. I felt the baby's movements. I felt him trying to come out. I made a great effort. I breathed deeply, contracted my whole body, breathed again, pushed with all my strength, and suddenly the head was in the midwife's hands, the shoulders, the behind, the legs. I heard a strong cry. My baby was outside. He was crying.

Exhausted and wet with perspiration, I lay on the bed. The nurse laid the baby next to me, wrapped in a nappy, without one word.

I was a mother.

I breathed deeply, touching my new son gingerly. He was so helpless. Small and pink. I kissed him gently, looked at him and cried. His hands were red. He'd worked so hard to come out into the world. I opened his fingers, and they gripped my finger. His cheeks were flushed, but he had red and blue marks around his eyes. It had been cramped for him inside the womb.

How would I leave here with him, with the yellow patch on me? I was so afraid.

I was exhausted. I slept most of the day. Occasionally I nursed the baby, and after he had drunk his fill I went back to sleep. I was weak and in pain. It was hard for me to sit, and hard for me to walk. My breasts were swollen and painful. What would tomorrow bring?

I waited for night. I had decided to escape the hospital as quickly as I could. The scenarios in my head were horrible. I was afraid of collaborators with the Nazis who would be likely to help with solving 'the Jewish problem', who would plot against me and my baby.

Night. Quiet all around. I wrapped the baby in a blanket. I tiptoed out of the hall where the new mothers slept. I opened the door, and went out into the hospital courtyard. Utter silence surrounded me. No one around. I decided to walk towards the streetcar. At this hour there would be no passengers.

Someone came out of the bushes. I was startled. My heart pounded. I had a baby. I knew I must protect him at all costs. Then I sighed in relief. Unbelievably, Mittyu was holding me to him. He took the baby in his arms and cried. My big, handsome husband was crying tears of happiness. Mittyu had become a father.

All the fear, pain and weakness flowed away through a release of tears, tears I tried to conquer. Mittyu held me to him, and the baby between us.

'My Shoshana a mother. And I a father...'

Quietly we walked towards the streetcar. I was losing strength. One step more, one step more and I would faint. Mittyu held the baby in one arm and supported me with the other. We were already in the streetcar. We were both wrapped in the blanket I had taken from the hospital, and the baby was between us. A few Gentiles got on, and looked at us suspiciously. What had we done to them? Why this hate?

We had arrived. We got off and walked under cover of darkness. My steps were slow. I had no more strength. At last we had come 'home', to the camp, to the stench of the hotel. The guard looked at us in wonder when he heard the baby crying. Perhaps he even smiled. He opened the gate for us without a word.

I was now in a room with some other girls. The baby was next to me. Mittyu stayed by me for a long time. He stroked me and the baby. I was wet with a cold sweat. I nursed the baby, and fell asleep as he was nursing. In the morning the girls awoke to the sound of the baby's cry. What a commotion. What joy! They were excited. I saw only love around me. It was a pity that my mother and father could not share in our joy.

I turn off the cassette. I am so deep into the story that it seems that I can smell the baby. A soft, pink baby, with tiny hands and plump legs. A baby in a hotel seething with hate.

I think of my sister Shiri. When she was born and they brought her home the house was fragrant with flowers. Shiri slept in a soft bed, with an abundance of toys around her and a colourful mobile playing above her head. There was a lovely atmosphere in the house when my brother, Rotem, was born, too. Pleasant aromas, cheerful colours, grandparents, aunts and uncles, many friends, guests, gifts and flowers, and music coming from the stereo system. And when Tali came home with Ima, there was no end to the joy. We all received the tiny baby with warmth and love.

Reiseleh has a baby too, but there everything is grey and cold. I need to digest all this. Again I look through the faded album, and I see a picture. A good-looking man and woman wearing festival clothes. It seems the woman is Reiseleh. The man is holding a plump, smiling baby, a ribbon tied in a butterfly shape on her head. I am able to figure out some of the words on the back of the picture: Sheindele, Chaim, Miriam. Chaim is Great-grandmother's brother, and this is his wife. She really is like Reiseleh. And the baby is so sweet. Miriam is her name? Where is she now? I must figure out the mysteries. What does Ima always say? 'A bit of patience won't hurt you.' So I breathe deeply, and turn the cassette back on and listen to Grandma Reiseleh once more.

13
Three Babies

We decided to call the newborn 'Gidon'. We wanted him to be a hero, like Gideon from the Bible, who was able to save Israel from the Midianites. Who knows? Perhaps our Gidon will save us from the fear embittering our lives.

As I nursed little Gidileh, I heard a knock on the door. Two beautiful young girls entered our shack. They brought a gift for our Gidi: a soft sky-blue suit of clothes. They looked at the baby and smiled. I turned to the two friends and thanked them very much for the gift. I promised that our Gidi would wear the clothes he received from them the day we boarded the ship that would take us to Israel.

'From this day on call me Shoshana,' I asked everyone. 'I want to put off all signs of the exile. From now on I am the mother of a child who will grow up free and happy in Eretz Israel.'

Mittyu's voice now comes from the cassette.

Shoshana stayed in the shack. She had stopped working because of the nursing. I went on working. My back ached unbearably from working as a porter. They were taking advantage of us. My muscles hurt. From morning till night, under threat from Slovak officers, I lugged, dragged and pulled. One Slovak officer came every morning with a terrifying black dog with a wrinkled face and razor-sharp teeth. Woe to whoever rested, even for one minute. A friend of mine, Vlovaleh, put down the piano he was carrying on his back to rest for a minute, and stood up. When he prepared to lift the piano again, the Slovak officer made the dog attack him.

I carried on working, like a machine. When things were hard for me I thought of my Shoshana and my Gidon. As I 'saw' them and forgot all the hardships, the load was lighter.

Gidon's eyes were as blue as the sky, just like my Shoshana's. He was already smiling, and his smile melted away all the hardships. When I returned in pain, exhausted and hungry, I rested by Shoshana with the baby between us. I told Shoshana what had happened, in a whisper, and asked her to watch and listen. I wanted to know what had happened to my friend. I was worried about him.

I looked at our son's golden hair that had just begun to grow, and I melted. Gidon was our little prince. A child of gold. He was so good. Most of the time he was quiet and calm, and we called him Gidi and Gidileh as pet names.

He had just finished nursing. He nursed with spirit, and Shoshana had plenty of milk, thank God. I took care to bring her part of my food ration. She had to eat well. It was important to me that she had milk to nurse our boy.

About two weeks after Gidi was born another 'guest' came to the women's shack. A baby girl. So now there were three babies in the hut. Yitzhakleh, Gidi and Rivkaleh. Hanna, the new mother, was pleasant, but so weak. The baby cried so much and the mother tried to calm her in whatever way possible. She was at Hanna's breast day and night, but still she screamed.

The women in the room began to grumble. Coming back after a gruelling day's work, tired and full of worry, they wanted to rest a bit, and the baby was wailing. Shoshana pitied the mother and the other women, and asked for the baby for a minute. She put the baby to her breast, and the little one grew calm at once. The baby drank thirstily, and then lay peaceful and at rest till she fell asleep. From that day Shoshana nursed both babies. First Gidi, and after he had fallen asleep, she would nurse Rivkaleh.

Hanna and her husband couldn't thank my Shoshana enough. They brought her some of the food they received, so that she would stay strong and have enough milk for both babies. Gidon and Rivkaleh developed slowly, and as for Yitzhakleh, he was already a big boy at six months old. The babies' smiles gave me much strength. I thought of these smiles during the hard times, and was encouraged.

I so admire these grandparents. They were so young, and life was so demanding. A horrible war raging around them, they didn't know what was happening with their families, what was happening with Reiseleh's ill mother; she needed insulin every day; who would bring it for her from the chemist? Reiseleh's father's livelihood must have been damaged because of all the new laws and limitations, and her brother, Chaim, had a wife and a baby to care for. I know that one of the Nuremberg laws forbade making any purchases at Jewish shops. The Germans took care to mark these shops and businesses so that everyone would keep from buying or trading with the 'dirty' Jews. Did they also mark Shmuel Grinfeld's coffeehouse? Was Helinka still studying at the secondary school? Did Shoshana and Mittyu have any idea what was going on at home?

> True, I had work, and Shoshana had a roof over her head and enough milk to feed our son. But fear paralyzed us all. Vlovaleh was lying in the shack, his body lacerated. Luckily there was a doctor there who was able to care for the wounds on his body and his face. His groans made me angry. If I could, I would have strangled that evil Slovak officer and his dog with my own hands. Would Vlovaleh go back to work? The babies' smiles calmed my anger somewhat. All this was accompanied by the endless waiting for the passport. We all waited with expectation to receive the passport that would save us, in order to finally set out and immigrate to the Land.

On Shabbat I ask Grandpa Gidi and Grandma Aliza to go and visit Yosef again. Uncle Yosef had been in the same hotel as my great-grandparents. I heard from my parents that he spends most of his time now writing his memoirs of that time. I have so many questions to ask him. Yosef is a primary source. He will tell me what they went through there.

14
Chaim, Sheindele, a Baby and an Aunt

We are at Yosef's house again, sitting on his balcony, and the winter sun strokes us with pleasant warmth. Yosef, in spite of his advanced age – more than eighty – is still very vital. He remembers places, dates and happenings, and tells of them as though they happened yesterday.

Grandma Aliza has received many pages he has written, in which he tells the family history and what happened during the war. She has photocopied all the pages, and is now giving the originals back to him.

Yosef goes to the kitchen and makes tea for us. I look around. There are pictures of his children and grandchildren everywhere. A picture of his Dinchu, may her memory be a blessing, is on the television. We drink, and Yosef talks. I sit quietly. I don't want to interrupt the flow. Yosef is now talking about Chaim, Reiseleh's brother.

'Yes, I met Chaim in the *hachsharah* platoon in Ulmitz. He came there with his wife and the baby. I was there too before I came to Prague. He was waiting for the immigration permit for Israel as well.

'One day he received a letter from home: "My Chaim. The situation is very bad. The illness is eating me up."'

Chaim decided to return home with his wife and the baby. I remember him, a tall and handsome young man. He could have been a film actor. When I last met him we discussed the political situation. We heard and knew that the Germans were acting as they wished in the conquered territories. Many Jews had been exiled from their homes, but we did not know where. We hoped that Chaim would return to Bushtina and find his parents there.'

Yosef is lost in thought for many long minutes.

'Yosef, here is a letter from Gitale, Chaim, Reiseleh and Dinchu's mother.' Grandma Aliza hands Yosef the letter. It's one I found in the suitcase; one Ima has had reconstructed. Yosef looks at the letter, written in Hungarian, reads excitedly and translates at once.

My dear daughters,

I hope my letter finds you strong, happy and healthy. We sent you a letter which told that Chaim has a daughter. She is lovely.

A few days ago Chaim was drafted to a work camp in Plashov. We hope that he will come back safely. His wife, Sheindele, her sister, Rita, and the sweet baby too, now live with us. Abba has no work, and life gets harder from day to day.

I am angry with myself about the letter I wrote to Chaim at Ulmitz. Rita was also with them in the camp. She thought that it would be easier for her to return to London to her husband from there. I have brought evil on them with my own hands.

Luckily you did not obey me; I am happy that you, at least, are not here.

Destiny laughs. Chaim has come here from Ulmitz, from the *hachsharah* camp, and was immediately sent by the Germans to the work camp in Plashov. I've heard hard things about this camp. I've heard that the boys work their hearts out in forced labour, even to death. I only hope that Chaim will have sufficient strength to endure there.

The only light in my life is little Miriam. She is always cooing and laughing, and her eyes are full of light.

A week ago, all the women and babies were taken away from the village next to ours. The Germans explained that it is for 'resettlement'. At our age, to resettle? What are we, pioneers? I hope it doesn't come to us.

In the meantime, Sheindele and Rita are helping me. They do all the housework. They buy insulin for me out of their savings. Sheindele is a good woman, and her sister, Rita, is like an angel in heaven for us. Sometimes I mistakenly call her Reiseleh. She reminds me of you, my little girl. May God grant her only good.

It is truly a pity that we stood in your way. You were right. I hope that the permit to get on the ship to Israel will come quickly.

Take care of yourselves, my sweet girls. I miss you so, and pray to God that you will have only good. You cannot imagine how happy I was when we received a letter from you, and we learned of our two new grandchildren. Continue writing, please.

Give our greetings to your husbands, and hearty kisses to Yitzhakleh and to Gidon. I hope to have the privilege of seeing the two little men who have been added to the family. We want to have the privilege of embracing them both.

We hope for better days. I am giving the pen to Abba. He too wants to write.

My dear daughters,

I believe you have done the right thing. May HaShem [God] keep you from all evil. When you arrive in the Holy Land, try to do all you can so that perhaps we also could join you. It would be good if you could use connections to expedite the process to get permits for us. I pray for Chaim's welfare.

How could it have been helped? We needed his help here. If we had not written to him at the *hachsharah* camp, he would of course have stayed with Sheindele, her sister and tiny Miriam, and most likely would have made aliyah with his family to Israel.

To our sorrow, he has been sent to Plashov. We hope he will return well from there. Amen.

Take care of yourselves, our dear daughters, take care of your husbands and of our grandchildren.
A warm, fervent kiss to each one of you,
I love, embrace and bless you.

Yours, Abba.

Yosef finishes reading. He looks at us in silence. I want to ask questions, but I am silent. What happened to Chaim? What happened to his wife, and to little Miriam? What happened to Rita and Grandma's parents?

I look at Yosef and ask at last: 'Do you know what happened to them?'

Yosef's face is pale. It is hard for him to speak. We are silent too.

Yosef turns to me: 'Roni, you need to write a "roots" project. Your roots are so deep. You have so much to write. Maybe we should let your question go? It's hard for me to tell you. You're still too young for this."

'Uncle Yosef, I may be young, but it's important to me to know the whole truth. Yes, I might be sad. But don't you think you need to tell? We must know what happened there. Even the history teacher has spoken with us about the importance of learning the events. Perhaps we can learn from the experience of that terrible war, and so prevent things like this happening in the future?'

Deep lines appear in Yosef's forehead. His eyes blaze.

'I know much about the Shoah ['calamity' – the Holocaust]. I've read much. I am interested and ask questions. I've seen films, even those that document the horror. I've heard live testimonies on television and at school. They speak with us about these things before Holocaust Day. So don't you think I need to know what happened to my family?'

Yosef looks at Grandpa Gidi and Grandma Aliza to 'get their permission'. I understand the looks.

Again there is a long pause. Tension is in the air. I see Grandpa Gidi wiping a tear from the corner of his eye, almost absentmindedly, so no one will notice. Yosef raises his head. He looks at me with his deep brown eyes. It seems he must organize his thoughts. I feel that it is painful to him, as though he is opening a wound that has already closed.

After a long silence Uncle Yosef says that one day in Ulmitz he met a girl from Bushtina. Her name was Miraleh. She told him that she had been evicted with the children, the women and the elderly. Beside her walked Gitale and Koppel.

> Snow was falling and there was frost. Gitaleh felt ill on the way. Her husband Koppel walked beside her. His white beard trembled from weakness and cold. He attempted to support Gitale, but his strength was not sufficient. Gitale sat down on the side of the road and took out a syringe from her hidden bag. She had to inject herself with insulin. Her hand shook from cold and weakness. The syringe broke. Half of it remained stuck in her leg. We went on walking. Gitale and Koppel grew very weak. Their steps slowed. It was clear to me that they would not survive. Their faces were full of fear. And then we heard the terrifying barks of dogs, coming closer and closer. Koppel looked at me and pleaded that I run.
>
> 'You must save yourself. Don't worry about us.'
>
> I ran as long as my strength lasted, spurred on by terror. There they remained, on the road.

'There.' Yosef wipes his forehead. 'I know no more. I don't know what happened to the rest of the family.'

Grandma Aliza embraces me warmly. How I need that hug now. I struggle against tears. I had just announced that I was strong and mature enough to hear everything. But when I see the tears in Yosef's eyes, in Grandma's eyes, in Grandpa Gidi's eyes, I start to cry. We all weep, without shame. In fact, why be ashamed? Grown-ups can cry too.

How good it is that Reiseleh and Dinchu left home in time. What luck.

From this whole family, only they were left. The Scheiner sisters did not find one other member of their family, in spite of searches and communications.

Now I understand better the last words of Grandpa Gidi's eulogy to his father: 'We are here because Abba was right.'

15
At Last

How wonderful it is that I have good friends. Ever since we received the assignment to do the 'roots' project we talk a lot and review important, exciting and hard things about what happened to our families. Dorit's grandparents have an amazing story of bravery and illegal immigration from Morocco. Moran has a particularly hard story of illegal immigration from Syria. Her grandfather made *aliyah* from Syria when he was a child; he came on foot with a group of children. She tells me of the dangers that beset the children till they came to a kibbutz on the shores of our Jordan.

I think a lot about what happened to our people. A terrible war, under the shadow of boundless illogical hate, and here in the Land wars, hunger, the Mandate government limiting *aliyah*, illegal immigration in horrible conditions… and in spite of all this we have a country. This country was not given to us on a silver platter, as poet Nathan Alterman wrote. Now I understand better the poem we learned in class.

I've been corresponding through the computer with Noa, Petr's granddaughter. He was my great-grandfather's and Grandpa Gidi's adopted brother. No, I still don't know how, why, when. Again I say to myself: patience, patience. I must meet Petr. Noa cannot tell me everything. I also don't want to press her too much. In the beginning I ask unendingly: who adopted your grandfather? Why? When was that? Does he have a connection with his adoptive parents? What happened to his parents, did they abandon him? I feel that my questions are annoying her. She hints to me that it would be best if I met her grandfather myself, and she also would be happy to meet me at his house.

At that very moment Ima comes home with my brother and sisters.

There is noise and joy at home. Only I am thoughtful. The question that frustrates me is, why was Petr adopted and why is his name Grinfeld? Is he a brother of Grandpa Gidi? And if so, why is Grandpa Gidi not called Grinfeld?

At our family dinners, I don't stop asking and being interested but I don't mention the name Petr. I don't want to tell them what I already know… I try to get a few more crumbs of information about what my great-grandparents went through. How wise they were when they recorded what happened to them. When I hear the cassette it seems that they are still with us.

I rummage through the tattered suitcase. Ima has already taken out all the letters that can be reconstructed. Maybe I will still find something else. This suitcase is my hidden treasure. Again I see the white pacifier. What is it hiding? How is it connected to my 'roots' project?

Again I am at Grandpa Gidi's house. We have finished eating, and I can still taste the orange I picked from the tree. I look at Grandma. She is always active, and has interesting hiding places, hidden paths she takes me on and where she shows me special things. She already has so many wrinkles, giving away that she isn't so young anymore…

Grandma has started telling me about her trip to Poland. She went with a delegation of young people that she had taught some years before. Noa has told me that Petr also joins student trips to Poland a lot, as a man of witness.

'Petr has an amazing survival story. He is often hosted in schools so that he can tell the students what he has seen. In a few more years, you also can join student trips there.'

'What, Petr is a man of witness? He was so young.'

'Yes, Petr was there, in Auschwitz. A boy of four.'

'A boy of four? He couldn't work and be useful for the German war effort.'

'Petr was the youngest child in the camp. He was... I think it's better that Petr should tell.' Again Grandma is hiding the answers. I look at her. She looks thoughtful to me. This journey to the valley of death affects her very much.

'What can I say? Only there, on that cursed earth, can we understand even slightly what happened in that horrible war. Only there, perhaps, you can connect to what happened to Grandpa Gidi's parents and their family, and what happened to Petr.'

I already know: I will go there when the time comes. In the meantime I must continue to fish out everything possible from anyone who is available.

In the meantime, Noa is my faithful source of information. Grandma promises me that I will meet Petr. But when? In the class a few 'roots' projects are already ready, having been written by students who are particularly quick. And I, I am still at the beginning of the work. Yonit, my teacher, has given me as long an extension as is necessary. She knows I have a lot to write. When I spoke with her she was very excited when I told her what I am doing.

'My project will be very, very big,' I reported to her. 'I've dug too deep, and I've got all the way to my grandparents' grandparents.'

And this is only one branch among other branches I have. I also want to know about Grandma's family and about my father, Eran's family. But I can't cover everything. I've already decided that I will only research one branch for this project. I will write about the other branches for myself when I have time. I know I will do this.

The cassette is before me again. Grandpa Mittyu's voice comes from it.

> We were in the camp for temporary workers for about two months. We have no pleasant memories of this place. In spite of the Slovak and German officers' humiliations, we did everything to keep our humanity.
>
> One Friday afternoon, right when we were preparing to receive Shabbat, the man who was responsible for getting the permits came to us. His smile made everything clear. The *aliyah* permits for the ship that would bring us to Eretz Israel had come at last.
>
> Group by group we prepared to receive Shabbat. The candles burned this time with a particularly shining light. We were all full of hope that the end of our troubles had come. So we thought.
>
> I held the permit I received with trembling hands. This paper would bring us to our true home. I knew many of the permits were forged. Each such permit saved lives, and if it needed to be forged, they would forge it, if by so doing they could save as many as possible.
>
> Shoshana gave little Rivkaleh into her mother's arms. She fell asleep during nursing and seemed happy and full. Gidi too, who was already two months old, slept the sleep of the just. The babies were content, and there was quiet in the shack. Reiseleh looked at the permit, and it seemed she had difficulty understanding that it was real. Immediately she took two suitcases out from under the bed: the little brown suitcase, with all the pictures and letters, and one more big suitcase. She began packing, and I helped her. In two more days we would be at sea.
>
> The door opened. Hanna's husband came in. He looked happy. They had also received the permit they hoped for. Many of the people in the hotel had received it and the joy was great. Hundreds

of people were happy now. The hope for a good life, a life of freedom, of work and of joy, shone a great light into everyone's hearts.

Reiseleh and Hanna took the dirty sheets off their beds. They tore the sheets into squares, and divided the squares between them. These would be the nappies on the journey.

16
Setting Out

The room is quiet. Only the cassette makes a small noise. Grandma clears her throat.

> It is hard to describe what happened in the room during those two days. Hanna and I thought about each thing, about anything that could help us during the voyage. One more rag, one more piece of blanket, one more sleeveless shirt. Even a few old biscuits went into the suitcase. In a minute the suitcase would explode! I wrote in big white letters on the two suitcases: 'Grinfeld'.
>
> We came to the shores of the Danube, the anchorage of the river ship *Helius*. We tried to be always together: Mittyu, I and our Gidi; Jutyu; Hanna, her husband and baby Rivkaleh; Dinchu, Yosef and Yitzhakleh. Next to us stood many other excited people from among the ones who were with us at the hotel, and a few refugees as well who had succeeded in coming here from the extermination camp Buchenwald a few days before – emaciated, their eyes sunken in their sockets, the clothes on them torn and tattered.
>
> My heart almost stopped beating. Gestapo officers oversaw the embarking on to the boat. Lines of policemen surrounded us, and rifles were aimed at us. The Germans did everything to frighten the refugees, so that we should not dare to return to German Reich territory.

The ship set out. The joy that filled us was mixed with fear. It seemed an eternity until we arrived at the Romanian port of Tolchea. The steeples of the impressive churches looked at us, backed by grey sky, and the sound of ringing bells was clear and sharp.

In Tolchea three freight ships were waiting for us. We had waited for them for two months in the stench of that hotel. During this time people laboured to repair the three hulks that were meant to take us to Eretz Israel. Two of them were small ships, the *Pacific* and the *Milus,* and one was bigger – the *Atlantic.* Hundreds of illegal immigrants crowded into the small ones. Each one carried a suitcase or a small parcel in his hand, but no more. We were limited to a small amount of personal baggage only. I hoped I would not be obliged to throw away any of our 'great possessions'. The two small ships were already setting sail. Our turn had not yet come. A little time passed and the instruction came to board the *Atlantic.* The crowding was great. The ship was almost overloaded…

Gidi was wearing his sky-blue suit. His blue eyes shone, but only for a short while. Amidst the terrible crowding, the illness and filth, I saw the young girl who had brought Gidi the first gift of his life. She took care to visit me and little Gidon, who was lying on the bunk, ill … She said to me again and again: 'This baby gives me much strength.' Oh, I wish my memory didn't betray me. I don't remember her name. Wait a moment, I've remembered, her name is Annina! Yes, Annina.

Grandpa Mittyu continues:

It is unbelievable. We, 1,800 illegal immigrants, crowded onto the *Atlantic.*

Eichmann, the one who was Hitler's right hand and head of the Jewish branch of the Gestapo, did not oppose us and even helped the Jews leave the Reich territory. By so doing he thought to help the Nazis solve the 'problem' and get rid of as many Jews as possible. He must have been sure that these hulks would never reach their destination.

The illegal immigrants continued crowding into the ship. Each immigrant took as few personal goods as possible. There was no place for extras on this rickety ship. Even the physical weight of the passengers had already passed the permitted weight. Shoshana gave up many things, but she took the letters with her. She gathered them in a tin and put them on the bottom of the little suitcase. When we were boarding and finding our place, each one on his narrow bunk, news came that the Germans were committing pogroms against the Jews of Romania. The Jews in the cities of Iassi and Bucharest were victims of abuse, but it was not known exactly what was happening there. If only we could succeed in eluding the pogroms that had already come this far. We were all assisting in the last preparations before weighing anchor. We loaded the ship with parcels: boxes of dried onions, rusks, water tanks, sugar, tea, and two big boxes labelled 'Emergency', food for hardship, and rescue equipment and life jackets had been loaded as well.

We were certain that the journey would take a week, perhaps two weeks at the most. Everyone was urging the ship's crew to set out, but they were not moving. They were waiting. Knowing that the ship was rickety, that it was very crowded, that British soldiers were waiting in ambush for each ship, they were not hurrying to leave. Illegal immigrants who came to the coast of Eretz Israel were being chased away, and the crew were likely to pay for it themselves as well. So in spite of all this, how would we still get them to leave?

Lazarkeh, an emaciated young man, but young and spirited, a refugee who succeeded in escaping Buchenwald by the skin of his teeth, was the clever one. He organized contributions. He and two other men who were chosen to be on the illegal immigration committee called upon us all to contribute what we could. People stood in line to give their contribution. Women took off their wedding rings. Reiseleh said goodbye to the ring that Mother Gitale had given me to give to her. Dinchu wiped away a tear and took off the necklace that was engraved with a dedication from their parents. The men also queued up. They gave the little money that they had been able to save.

When the five crew members saw the parcel of money and jewellery, they shook the hands of the ship's committee, and the bargain was struck. The ship weighed anchor, and the illegal immigrants shouted 'hurrah'.

17
Hard, Hard, Hard

When we had set out, we took care to raise the Panama flag to trick the British who were waiting for us at every point. I decided to walk around and check the condition of the creaking ship. I went into the engine room, and could not believe my eyes. Everything looked old and neglected, the walls were eaten by rust and were crooked. On the lower deck I saw four narrow wooden doors. They led to primitive and neglected water closets. Rats scampered on the floor with no one bothering them, the sewage pipes were blocked, and a horrible stench arose not long after we had set out. A rusty iron sign said: 'Ship's weight: 1,500 tons'. By quickly calculating, I found out that a ship like this was permitted to carry some three hundred people. In fact, six times that number had crowded in. Once I had seen what the true situation was, I started to worry.

A Gestapo boat continued to accompany the ship out into the sea. They knew better than anyone what the ship's real condition was. The three ships had waited in a shipyard, and had been intended for scrapping. However, those responsible for the illegal immigration were happy about this 'find' that had fallen into their hands. It was better than nothing, and so these hulks became a true treasure. The institutions that acted for *aliyah* had collected funds from Jews around the world and paid much money to the government of Greece for them. Greece, which was still neutral, then, in the war, was preparing for hard days and was happy to be rid of them in return for a much-needed good sum of money.

On the way we had to anchor in one of the ports to take coal on board, but no country allowed us to approach its shores. All the countries had divested themselves of their duty to help, even in return for money.

Mittyu, enough about the ship. It's best if you let me tell about what was in the ship.

Reiseleh sounds impatient. She begins:

So, as you said, the crowding was intolerable. I pushed and shoved those standing before me with Gidi in my arms. I protected him so that he should not be crushed, a small baby, only two months old, and immediately took possession of the bunk that had been given me. The narrow bunks were ordered in banks of three. I received a bunk on the lowest level because of the baby. Gidon slept the sleep of the just. He was so easy… Suddenly I felt horrible nausea. I left Gidi on the bunk and ran to the washroom.

A long queue had already formed and the stench was intolerable. I was choking, but I waited quietly. My belly turned over inside me and I was afraid I would have to vomit. I understood immediately that order and discipline were real necessities here. It was forbidden to complain or shove people.

In order to follow the rules, a committee had been chosen to take care of problems that arose. Mittyu was one of the members. All the passengers had agreed to follow the committee's instructions. After one day of sailing, many had already fallen ill. Some of them spent their time in the toilets, others lay on their bunks, exhausted. When Gidi fell asleep, I wanted to shower. Maybe the shower would ease me and calm the nausea.

The shower was of seawater only. My skin burned. When I had revived a little I also washed Gidi. His skin also burned from the salt. I therefore only 'spoiled' him rarely with a shower. I would dip the nappy in the meagre cup of water that I had received to drink that day, and with that rag I would clean all of him. Even though his skin was burned, Gidon was calm…

I hear Grandpa Mittyu's cough. He continues from here:

I was among those who had been tasked with helping the crew maintain the ship during the voyage. The Greek crew knew well that they were likely to be blamed for taking illegal immigrants. They did not stop complaining: 'The work is harder than we thought. The danger is great. The coal is not sufficient. The stench bothers us.'

We all knew they were likely to prove an obstacle to the illegal immigration; to turn back, to delay, or to do all sorts of tricks so as not to stand trial by the British. We had to speak to them over and over again. There was not one immigrant on the ship who did not put his hand into his pocket again to 'calm' the crew and spur them on to navigate towards the shores of the Land. In spite of this we knew that we had to stand guard. They could prove an obstacle to the voyage at any moment.

The crew did do all they could to postpone the arrival. They navigated our hulk from island to island. The routes were well-known to them; it was only we who did not know where we were being led. We had no map or compass. Each piece of land was a mystery to us. We stood on guard. One of us even had a pistol for emergencies.

I did not sleep at night. I was like a coiled spring. I lay down close to the engine room … I carried great responsibility on my shoulders. I must do everything to ensure that we arrive in Israel safely.

18
Frustrating Questions

I turned off the cassette player. It's hard for me to continue now. I must rest. I feel my heart stormy within me. How could this be? There in Europe the destiny of the Jews was set that they would be taken to extermination camps, and here the British close the gates of the Land? Why did the world not involve itself? What was the meaning of all the laws limiting immigration quotas? Why did the Jews not try to escape the claws of the Nazi beast and flee to other countries?

It becomes clear to me, after I ask and ask, that no country wanted to grant entrance to the Jews fleeing for their lives. I ask Ima to take me to Grandpa Gidi. I want to hear from him; maybe he will be able to answer the questions that frustrate me.

Grandpa Gidi looks at me with his azure eyes: 'My Roni. You are our oldest grandchild. I want you to be happy.'

'Grandpa, do not evade the issue this time! Do you think I will be happy if you avoid my questions every time?'

'My Roni, the things that happened were very hard. The Germans had a plan to get rid of the Jews. Hitler published a book that gave ideas to those who hate the Jews and to those who wrote the Nazi propaganda. The book stated that the Jews were the source of all the problems in Germany, that the Jews were a low race and that they needed to be got rid of.'

'Grandpa, I've already heard this and I know it very well.'

But it's as though Grandpa does not even hear me. He continues his explanations.

'The Germans' hate for the Jews became an illogical hate. The Nazi propaganda nourished it, and it became stronger from day to day. The Germans tried to get rid of the Jews in different ways even before the war. Already in 1937 Eichmann, the Nazi persecutor, had been sent to Israel to try to make an exchange with activists of the Jewish community there, the Yishuv. He promised them to allow German Jews to immigrate in their hundreds to Eretz Israel, and this in exchange for their money and possessions. They would leave everything in Germany, and come only with the clothes on their back. Many of the activists among the Yishuv here in the Land wanted to realize this exchange, but it did not take place. The British did not allow it. They took care to follow the "White Paper" instructions and allow Jews to enter the land in limited numbers only. The Mandate was in their hands, and they wished to keep the peace in the area, and not irritate the Arabs who opposed Jewish aliyah to Israel. Do you know, Roni, that Jews who tried to immigrate to America were returned to Europe by ship? Would you believe it that America, that big and enlightened country, would act this way? Some of the Jews immigrated to Russia. They came even as far as Kazakhstan, and there they were received.'

Interesting. Grandpa Gidi is telling me as though he is a history teacher. He can't tell me his personal troubles. He is so careful to not hurt me, and this annoys me.

Now I want to return to the cassette.

19
The Sea is Against Us Too

I listen to Grandma Reiseleh's voice.

Shouts and cries of children and babies could be heard amid the crowd. Many vomited, and the stench only increased. The ship did not stop rolling. Everyone tried to take hold of something. Each movement turned us all inside out. Those on deck tried to take hold of a ledge, a piece of wood, a railing or a step to be close to the side and empty themselves into the sea. But when strength wanes, control is lost, and the ship became filled with vomit and groans.

I lay on my bunk. I held the baby to me and gathered air into my lungs. I felt terrible dizziness. The sea around me seemed a monster. It was so big and immense and seemed as if it was cooperating with the forces of evil, with the Germans, with the British and with the countries of the world that locked their gates to us. It struck the sides of the ship with its mountainous waves, and the ship creaked and rolled, but slowly, slowly goes forward in the raging water.

Luckily I had a lot of milk. Gidi nursed and slept. I also nursed baby Rivkaleh. But my strength left me. There was nothing to eat on the ship. The daily food ration for each immigrant was dried onions, a mouldy piece of bread and a little water. Mittyu helped the Greek captain to navigate the ship. In return, each time, he would receive a beetroot. He brought me this treasure and we ate it in secret.

It was important to Mittyu that I eat. Two babies needed my milk. After I gnawed the sweet beetroot, I wiped the purple juice from my mouth and teeth with great care, so as to not give the secret away. Everyone was hungry.

The voice changes. Grandpa Mittyu continues:

The ship had no compass and no maps. How were we to steer? We were surrounded by water, lots of water. The sea was immense, and we had no idea which direction we were sailing in. The sun was the only landmark. There were some stars at night, if there were stars at all. The crew would shout: 'Everyone to the right', and we all moved to the right. And then: 'Quick, quickly to the left', or 'Everyone up'. Everything was accompanied by hand motions and raised voices. We did not understand their language, and they did not understand ours. Hand motions were the only language everyone understood.

Our second day in the heart of the Black Sea was the eve of the Day of Atonement. On the twelfth the *Atlantic* crossed the Dardanelles and anchored for a short time at Gallipoli. There the Turkish navigator left the ship. According to law only a Turkish navigator was licensed to guide the ship through the Aegean Sea. Shortly thereafter, the ship got into a terrible storm.

'We have sinned, we have transgressed, we are full of iniquity … Lord of forgiveness, you who see into hearts, you who revealed the deep things, you who speak righteousness, we have sinned before you, have mercy on us.' The men joined together in a downcast voice.

Lord of the world, how have I truly sinned? My greatest sin is that I am a Jew.

Grandma Reiseleh bursts into Grandpa's words:

And my great sin is that I left my parents and my brother, Chaim. I am a great sinner also.

Don't interrupt me, Shoshana. Do you remember the last meal before the Atonement Day fast? The children got sweet tea, and jam on their mouldy bread. Most of the men were on deck praying. Some aloud, some in a whisper: 'God, full of mercy.' The storm was raging in the sea. The huge waves crashed against the sides of our ship, threatening to break it to pieces. It swung from side to side, as though it too were praying. Towards evening one of the immigrants died. Lazarkeh, the spirited young man, got a high fever, could not stop vomiting, lost consciousness and died soon after.

Lazarkeh, the man who had succeeded in escaping the claws of the Nazis in Buchenwald, who was able to get to Bratislava, the man who was able to negotiate between us and the crew, he who volunteered for everyone's sake, found his death on the ship. From Lazarkeh's family not one small branch is left to continue the line.

I hear a choked groan. It is hard for Grandpa to tell about the hard time.

We placed Lazarkeh on a wooden plank. We wrapped him in a white sack, tied with a blue ribbon and a white ribbon, and two iron weights that we found in the engine room. Ten men recited the prayer for burial: 'God full of mercies, give him rest true rest on the wings of your indwelling presence…' After that… after that, we brought the plank to the rail of the ship, tilted it into the sea, and Lazarkeh's body slid into the depths. There he would find his rest.

There were many leaks in the ship. This was the time to check and repair as much as we could, to prepare for the rest of the voyage. The ship anchors again. We wanted to go ashore to rest a little bit, to recover from the nausea, to feel secure land under our feet, but the British boarded the ship, and the order that was given was unequivocal and unappealable: 'Leave here at once!'

Rumours raged among all the immigrants: 'The British are nervous. The Germans are annexing more and more pieces of the world to the Reich. Everywhere they get, they "clean" it of Jews. There is a great press of Jews who want to come to the Land. The British are tired, angry and frustrated.'

Again we sailed, now at the rate of six kilometres per hour. I, together with the immigrant committee, kept continual watch on the coal supply. My brother-in-law, Yosef, had joined the committee, to replace Lazarkeh. Worry gnawed at us. We were responsible here for so many men, women, children and babies; they were sick and hungry and hopeless. We made a hospital on deck and brought up the ill and dying. On deck the air was cleaner. They lay on their bunks, and this ship creaked beneath them, as though it were groaning and saying, 'Enough, I have no more strength to go on…'

Yosef and I stood guard over the food box meant for emergencies. The box was filled with sweet things: halva, sugar, jam. It was forbidden to open it. Two immigrants also guarded the water barrel. We guarded the food and the water day and night. We rationed one cigarette for each six guards to keep them from falling asleep on watch. They stood and inhaled the smoke of the cigarette one after another, each person in his turn.

We divided the water according to need. Those who were ill received a double portion. When I ended my nightly watch, I brought down scrap wood through the companionway into the furnace room. On the way I took hold of the steps, the rail, anything I could. The cargo in my hand slid away. I needed to overcome the rolls of the ship, to take good hold of the cargo and go on. I got to the engine room and vomited.

It was not terrible. In a minute I'd get to my bunk. I breathed deep breaths.

In the morning the storm grew stronger. It seemed that the sea breakers had all conspired to make game of us. A wave from the right, a bigger one from the left, and the biggest one from straight ahead. The ship creaked and rolled from side to side. Water came into the belly of the ship. Through all these rolls we had to gather materials to stop up the hole that had opened. Everything that could stop the cracks was collected immediately. Tatters of clothing, a rope, a rag, a piece of pipe. I and my friends worked madly. We emptied the water using cups and stopped up the cracks that opened again and again. If only we could reach shore. I prayed: 'God, now you must indeed be full of mercy.' No, it just couldn't be that after everything we'd gone through, the ship should sink.

The commotion was great; shouts, weeping, people vomiting, the captain shouting in any possible language: in Greek, in broken English, German, with hand and head motions, 'Go to the right, to the left, up', and the children crying.

And so the journey continued. Every hour we had a new challenge. We had to be alert and use every spark of thought and logic. We had to continue on and not give up.

The crew continued to navigate the ship from island to island, trying to make time and to delay the voyage to the desired goal. We reached the port of Piraeus. To our disappointment, the entrance into the port was barred with mines. We desperately needed more coal. All our attempts to communicate using the radio failed. Even the shouts of the crew did not help. There was no answer. And here, from between the rusty chains, came a pilot boat. This boat led us to the bay of Salamis, to a small port called Laurion.

Here we had a surprise: the representatives of the Jewish Joint Distribution Committee in Athens had instructed that the ship be loaded with baskets full of fresh bread, grapes, and even meat. Our eyes sparkled again with the light of hope. Everyone sat, wide-eyed and staring at the food that had come. We ate ravenously. I brought my Shoshana fresh bread and a bunch of juicy grapes. She smiled for the first time. She swallowed the bread, filled her mouth with grapes and gave me a look filled with thanks, love and hope.

This short rest helped us a little. We had gathered some strength for what was coming. We set out again, and the sea had no mercy. The ship sailed on terrifying waves. Again vomiting, again diarrhoea, again people were ill with a raging fever and with typhus, again desperation took hold of many. People lay on their bunks, their eyes dull. They tried to curl themselves up tightly, and choked down their groans.

Eight more people became ill and died. Again the shrouds and the blue and white ribbons. Again the *minyan* – the group of ten – and the burial prayer. The piston above the chimney blew a long blast, and we threw the body overboard. Maybe this sound would wake the One Who Sits on High to see our trouble? Maybe salvation would come from there?

Nine people had so far been cast into the depths of the sea. Nine souls floated above the ship as it drew nearer to the coast of the Land. They who evaded the horrible Holocaust, who were filled with hope when they boarded the ship, they who believed they would get to a safe haven, to the land of Israel, had been gathered into the heart of the sea, and they had not seen the Land, not even the coast before their eyes.

On board the *Atlantic*

20
The Ship Gets Stuck

Grandma Reiseleh spoke.

I was exhausted and dizzy, and continued to lie down and nurse, trying to preserve every drop of strength I had left. I took deep breaths to gather air in my lungs. I needed to calm down. I would still need much strength.

I'd lost count of the days. How long had we been at sea? Where were we? I was apathetic to everything happening around me. I waited in expectation for this nightmare to end. I heard whispers.

'Soon we will reach Cyprus.'

'Perhaps we can get off this coffin.'

'Perhaps they will allow us some rest from the rolling of the ship?'

'We have been at sea for three months already.'

We wandered from island to island to renew the provisions of coal and food, and when we reached Limassol a string of mines awaited us there as well. Here too the shore was blocked to us.

A British officer boarded the ship, accompanied by two sergeants. They looked pleased. Their uniforms were perfectly ironed, they were shaven and perfumed, their eyes scrutinizing the passengers and glancing suspiciously at everyone. We were all exhausted, hungry and despairing. British policemen came on deck and joined the officer and his men. They were frowning.

'Again illegal immigrants,' muttered their commander through his perfectly groomed mustache. 'How on earth are we to be rid of this problem?'

Mittyu, please continue, I'm thirsty.

The evening had already fallen and darkness enveloped the island. A blackout order was given. Even the boats were darkened. Long beams of light from huge searchlights lit the sky. Who was activating the searchlights?

My friends and I stood by the British commander and attempted to explain: 'We are not intending to get to the land of Israel. We will continue through the Suez Canal to the Indian Ocean. We have only strayed a little bit from our path in order to re-provision ourselves with food and coal. We must disembark for a little while.'

But the frowning officer did not let us disembark in Limassol.

'You were breaking the Mandate laws,' he said to us angrily. 'The *aliyah* to Palestine is forbidden by Mandate law. I cannot allow you to break a law.'

We tried to soften him with heartrending words:

'There are Jews here who have escaped the jaws of the Nazi beast in Czechoslovakia.'

'This boat is completely paid for. It is now our property.'

'All we want is to get to a safe haven.'

'We are escaping from death, from Hitler's claws.'

'It was Lord Balfour who gave the declaration permitting us a national home in the land of Israel.'

'We must escape. Death is chasing us.'

'We are refugees of war. We…'

The immigrants tried to distract the British policemen with arguments. We raised our voices, but the officer was adamant: 'You must obey the laws. It is impossible that you should do whatever you want.'

Additional boats came to the shore. A big British sailing ship was unloading cotton brought from Egypt. Ships sailed in, and boats were making their way to the quays. We saw British guardsmen armed with rifles. The British soldiers continued to walk the deck, and it was apparent that they were very angry. We heard that Italian planes, being allied with Nazi Germany, had bombed Athens a few hours before. Perhaps Cyprus was also in danger?

My friends continued to argue. The officer looked like he was about to lose his senses. He shouted, and the immigrants shouted in return. Under cover of the ship's movement and the intensity of the argument I escaped with some friends from the ship.

We came on shore and succeeded in smuggling coal into the ship. Jewish merchants in Limassol helped us with the loading and with a monetary contribution as well, in order to purchase the coal.

This was it. The British officer left our ship overcome with fury. Could it be that it was only a charade? The jewellery that was given to him secretly had apparently done its job.

At last I could go and rest a little. I lay on my bunk listening to the groans of the ill. The waves did not rest for a second. They rolled our ship mercilessly. I had to rest a little. Who knew what other surprises were waiting for us?

That night I heard a strange sound on the ship. I got up from my bunk and went on deck. The Greek crew stood close to the rail and… I rubbed my eyes to be sure that I wasn't dreaming. Had they gone mad? What were they doing? I saw them throwing the coal into the sea, the precious coal we had bought with the remaining money we had. They were doing everything to delay our advancement towards the land of Israel! In spite of the agreement, in spite of the many jewels that we gave into their hands, after they had taken all the money that we were able to gather, they were breaking the agreement we had with them.

I roused everyone and told them what I had seen. A great commotion arose. What should we do? How could we continue without coal? The ship was stuck and could not continue sailing. I asked all the young men to help with the work. Whoever had a little strength left helped and together we sawed up all the furniture in the ship. The ship groaned and cracked, and we continued to saw. This timber would be the fuel to move the ship and would enable us to advance to our desired destination.

The ship was limping again. Three days later, again the store of timber was finished. We sawed up an old piano, and then we sawed up the bunks that the immigrants had been lying on. First the bunks of the men, afterwards the bunks of the youth, and lastly the bunks of the women and children. They too were obliged to give up their beds.

The ship continued on its way and sailed through high waves. The autumn cold caused many immigrants to fall ill. We huddled together to share our warmth. The ill lay on the floor. With the rest of our strength we continued. We must not stop now. Each kilometre brought us closer to the goal. Slowly, slowly we advance.

The store of coal that fuelled the ship's engine slowly lessened. I went below decks to see what else could be sawed up. I saw one of the chairs that the crew had used. A little more, a little more…

The ship continued to advance through the Mediterranean Sea. We advanced in strong cold, through terrifying waves that threatened to swallow us. A little longer and we would reach shore. But suddenly the *Atlantic*, this ghost ship, stopped. It groaned, continued a few more metres, and stopped again. The coal was finished.

So, in the heart of the sea, between tempestuous waves, the ship was stuck and would not move.

There were many ill on the ship. Their apathy was devastating. Would we survive? What do you do with 1,800 immigrants on the ship?

The waves struck with all their strength. The creaks were dissonant in our ears. We attempted to tie down whatever could be tied with rope. We strengthened each screw. If only it did not fall apart. For six weeks the ship was stationary. No coal. The store of food also lessened. The crew was asleep. What did they care? Only the dysentery and the typhus cooperated with us. They were very active. More and more immigrants fell ill. We were helpless.

Sawing everything for fuel to move the ship

On the deck of the *Atlantic*

21
Dreams and a Surprise

I turn off the cassette player. It seems to me that I too am being shaken between the waves. I also feel nauseous. What is happening to me? I drink a cup of water. I breathe deeply. Abba has come.

'How are you? Roni, do you feel all right? You're a little pale. What's going on?'

'Abba, do you believe that it's possible to stay alive in this crowding? In the terrible starvation? To survive illness and exhaustion when the ship is rolling and people are vomiting? Can you believe that the immigrants gave all that they had to board the broken ship, hoping to get to the Land, and the crew took advantage of their hardship?'

Abba hugs me. 'Come on, Roni. Let's go outside for a bit, breathe some fresh air. You must calm down. Sometimes we need to take a break.'

We go into the garden. My siblings are there too. Running on the green grass, having fun in the little pool Abba has put in the garden. The sun is shining and its warmth caresses me. Abba gives me orange juice, and I drink it thirstily. How good it is here in our little house, in the green garden, with mischievous Shiri, with Rotem and with baby Tali. How good it is with my parents.

Uncle Yoav has come and brought my cousins with him in his jeep: Yahel, Idan, Gilad, Uri and Noam. How happy I am to see them. Tanned, happy, they run to me and give me a big hug. It's time for fun. We run on the grass, roll and are happy.

Uncle Yoav comes to me. 'So, how are you, Roni? I have something for you.'

'What? What is this?'

He gives me a large envelope. I open it and take out a big photo. Uncle Yoav has got the picture of the ship *Atlantic* from the archives of the Illegal Immigration Museum. He has enlarged the photo so that I can attach it to my paper.

'You're a great uncle,' I tell him.

Uncle Yoav is a career officer. He is away from home for long periods of time. He is fighting for our home here. I love him so much. I go back to my desk. Uncle Yoav joins me. He wants to listen to his grandparents. I turn the cassette player on. We hear Grandpa Mittyu's voice.

> In spite of this terrible suffering I said to Shoshana during a moment of desperation, 'Many people would be happy to be on our ship. There are entire families who will not get to Israel. After all this suffering we will reach a safe haven in the end. We will begin a new life, a life of freedom. Our Gidi will grow up to be a proud Jew, without fear, without a yellow patch on his sleeve.'
>
> I saw that my Shoshana was afraid. She looked at me with fearful eyes. I tried to encourage her. I sat next to her, I stroked her face and told her about the warm sun waiting for us and about the work in the kibbutz we would live in. I described how our work day would look in the field, in the cow shed, in the sheep pen, in construction, in the fragrant orchards. I described to my Shoshana the house I would build for her. A little house with a red roof, with a patch of grass and fragrant flowers in the garden. Gidi would be in the children's house, and there he would enjoy dedicated care, he would have enough food and many toys. I would build little toy wooden cars for the children's house, and…

Washing done in salt water drying on deck

I sat by Shoshana for a long time. I held Gidi when he cried, I changed his nappy for a stiff one that had been washed in salt water, and washed the dirty nappy with seawater. The baby's whole body was raw. A big red burn covered his behind. Gidi was not calm anymore. He was clearly suffering. All the babies cried often. I gave him his pacifier, but he still cried for a long time, until at last he calmed down and fell asleep.

I went back to stand next to the crew. I was watching over them as attentively as I could. The ship was stuck, and who knew what more damage this crew was likely to do.

The immigrants were apathetic. Their eyes were dull. They all lay exhausted and listless. The ill did not stop groaning, and the ship stayed still and did not move.

A British plane circled above us. Shortly thereafter a British towing ship arrived. Our ship was tied to it and we were towed to a nearby port. At last the needless stay at sea was ended. The British themselves had helped us. We received bread and water at port, and even coal. We set out again. From Cyprus the way was short. This time we were advancing towards the shores of the Land, with a British ship accompanying us.

The *Atlantic* nears land

    I wondered what happened to the two ships that went before us. Did they get to shore? Where were all the immigrants that were on them? Many strange thoughts assailed my mind. I was filled with hope, but with much worry also. Suddenly I saw ships drawing near. There were British soldiers on the ships. The ships surrounded ours. What would they do to us?

    They towed our limping ship towards the shores of Israel. The creaks of the ship did not scare me anymore. I didn't run to find ropes to tie and strengthen. In a little while we would be on shore.

    It was twilight now. The sun was about to set. The sky was painted crimson. It was late November. From a distance we could already see the Carmel Mountains, and white houses with red roofs on them. I gave all the immigrants blue and white ribbons that were in the box I had guarded. We all tied them on, some on lapels and some on forearms, everyone – even the ill, the despairing and the children. We flew the flag of Israel on the mast, and a great song burst from our throats. Even the ill joined in with sad voices. We all sang 'HaTikvah': 'Our hope has not yet been lost… To be a free people in our own land…'

    The young and strong among us started dancing in hora circles. Suddenly we had strength, and there was more room on the ship now too. Most of the bunks had been sawn up. One song and another song.

'Here in the land beloved of our fathers…'
'David, king of Israel…'
We danced in circles, excited, embracing and kissing each other.

By dawn we saw a big ship close to the shore. It was huge. On one of its sides we could clearly see the word *Patria*.

Who does this enormous ship belong to? we wondered, but we did not know the answer.

22
Sights of the City of Haifa... and also Oranges

British destroyers surrounded our limping ship. We heard the order from a British officer, 'Take the flag down from the mast!'

British police boarded the boat and surrounded the captain and his crew. We brought all our suitcases and possessions onto the deck, including the suitcase marked 'Grinfeld' in white letters. A British police boat circled our ship. The British had prepared for our coming. It seemed as though they'd already 'taken care of' the immigrants on the other two ships that came before us, and now our turn had come. Only afterwards we learned that those immigrants had been taken to the big British ship *Patria*.

The British sailors in the accompanying ship called to us on the loudspeaker: 'Anchor where you are. Do not approach the dock.'

The ship was stationary. Seeing the city of Haifa gave us a little hope. We were told that we would stay the night on the *Atlantic*. In the middle of that night I heard a sound. The sea was quiet. I got up and went over to the rail. I saw two figures trying to climb over it.

'We're Israeli,' they whispered. I looked at them suspiciously.

'I'm Dani.'

'And I'm Uzi. Help us up. We are from the Palyam, from the Haganah [underground army]. We have some information for you.'

Shaking from cold they came up on the deck. Their lips were blue. We helped them change into dry clothes we were able to collect.

Again new hope was kindled. The two young men would give us the information we needed. It was important to us to know what the British intentions were. The more details we knew, so we believed, the more efficiently we would be able to act. Dani and Uzi told us that Haifa had been attacked a few days before by Mussolini's army. The Italian army was fighting with the Germans against the Allies, and their planes had bombed Haifa. Their goal had been to strike the oil refineries that had been built in Haifa by the British.

'Look,' Uzi whispered to us, 'the British are losing their cool. The job they've been given here is too hard for them. They are not able to enforce the quota law they agreed on. The illegal immigrants are putting them to scorn. Immigrants are coming above and beyond the permits they have given.'

'Also,' Dani continued, 'the entire Yishuv in the Land laughs at their books of laws. The British are confused. Fighting on different fronts is beyond them. Now, when they have lost control, their senses have become dulled. They are cruel and treat immigrants as animals. "The law is above all", they state repeatedly, but we stay firm.

'The High Commissioner relies on the White Paper laws from May 1939, which are meant to limit Jewish immigration to the Land. The British will do everything to keep you from going ashore.'

More and more immigrants joined us and surrounded Dani and Uzi. They whispered a rain of questions to them in the dark of the ship.

'We will fight to the end. If we are condemned to death, we prefer to die in battle,' a few of the immigrants said. Tempers started to flare.

Uzi and Dani asked everyone to calm down.

'We have a plan. The Jewish Agency has already sent delegates to Washington and London to cancel the White Paper laws. The answer received from London was to segregate the immigrants who would come in camps until the end of the war.'

'Where are these camps?' we asked.

'Some are in Cyprus, others in Mauritius in the Indian Ocean, and one also at Atlit near Haifa. The British suspect that the Germans and their collaborators are putting Nazi spies among the illegal immigrants. We also know that the British have sent an order to the governor of the island of Mauritius to prepare a camp for receiving 4,000 refugees on three boats.'

'And you stayed silent? You will allow our deportation?'

'The commotion was great. I and my friends on the committee quietened the people.' Uzi continued:

'No, we did not and will not stay silent. Ben-Gurion [first prime minister of Israel] will not let this happen, nor will we. We all, the entire Yishuv in the Land have joined together to cancel this evil edict. People are demonstrating against the Mandate government's decisions all over the country. The immigrants who have already been moved from the boats *Milus* and *Pacific* to the British ship *Patria* are protesting as well. They have begun a hunger strike.'

'We won't allow it either. We will fight to the end,' came the calls from all over. 'We all, to the last of us, will physically resist. But if we need to, we will also fight.'

Dani and Uzi calm us. 'We won't let this happen. We will do everything to cancel the deportation order. We won't let them do as they wish with the immigrants.'

Dani continued: 'Pay attention. The British will tell you that they are putting all the immigrants on the *Patria* for sanitation – spraying, sterilizing, washing. They will tell you that the quarantine on their big ship will be 'only for two weeks', so that the doctors will be able to care for the refugees, and they will take care that all your needs will be met: food, drink, medicines and clothes. After two weeks, so they will tell you, you will be able to go ashore. We ask you: don't believe them. Fight. Another thing. Take care to check the oranges that they will bring onto your ship.'

Morning broke. A boat with food arrived, and a crate of oranges as well. Shiny bright oranges, a gift from our brothers in the Land. I look at the gift and immediately suspect a trap. I rummage between the beautiful oranges and find a note: 'Do not be afraid. Do all you can and resist boarding the *Patria*. Begin a hunger strike. We will do everything so that the deportation order will not be carried out. *Prepare for tomorrow*. Gather all your strength. Tomorrow everything will look different. Destroy this note immediately after reading it.'

Prepare for tomorrow? These words were particularly underlined. What will happen tomorrow?

We destroyed the note. Its contents were passed quietly from mouth to ear.

Another new morning, and we were still on the ship. We were all exhausted and helpless. A winter sun sent warm, pleasant rays. What waited for us today? It was already seven o'clock in the morning. I saw boats sailing towards our poor ship.

British soldiers boarded her. They searched our belongings and afterwards gave us a 'bait': halva, chocolate and other food that wakened our appetite. We did not touch the 'bait'. They brought crates of oranges onto the ship. No one touched this gold. We had declared a hunger strike.

The British sent more boats to our ship. Without warning, they forcibly dragged the women and the children and put them into the boats. Loud shouts and weeping were heard everywhere. The resistance was determined – kicks, raised hands and feet, but the soldiers overcame the exhausted women.

Two British soldiers went to Shoshana. Shoshana held on to Gidi with all her strength. She resisted and tried to kick the two soldiers holding her. She kicked and threw herself backwards, holding the baby tightly, but the soldiers overcame her. Shoshana and little Gidi were put on the boat. I could hear Shoshana's shouts even when the loaded boat drew away from our ship. The boat went towards the *Patria*. Hanna and baby Rivkaleh were put on that same boat too. I looked at the wake it left behind and shouted with all my strength, 'Shoshana, stand fast!'

The sound of despairing voices slowly weakened the further it got from the *Atlantic*. Other boats carrying British soldiers reached the ship. I was loaded forcibly onto a boat, and Yosef too, and Dina, and Yitzhakleh and Jutyu. We lay on the floor, kicking, shouting, but we could not overcome them. We struck the British soldiers with all the anger that had accumulated in us. The commotion was great. The waves struck the boat and tossed it as though it were a nutshell. The searchlights shone above us on the raging water.

We will not accept the evil deportation edict.

To all the Yishuv*! It has become known that all the preparations are in progress for deporting our brothers the illegal immigrants. The Yishuv will not rest until the evil edict is repealed! On Wednesday, 19 Marcheshvan 5701 (20 November 1940), from 12:00 until 24:00, **a general strike of the Hebrew Yishuv will take place,** signaling a demand to the authorities to allow our brothers the immigrants go ashore in the homeland. All members of the Hebrew Yishuv are called upon to cease their work in craft, industry, agriculture, trade and offices; school studies will cease; public transportation will be halted; cinemas, restaurants and places of entertainment will be closed! All who are employed by the military and the government, as well as those serving in medicine, lighting, water, etc. are relieved of their duty to strike. There will be complete order in the entire country. There will be no gatherings or processions. Each person in Israel is required to keep order. **We will not accept the evil deportation edict, nor will we be calm until the immigrants are brought ashore in the homeland. The Yishuv Guard.**

*Yishuv is the Hebrew term by which the pre-1948 Jewish community was known.

> I wanted to jump into the water. I knew how to swim. Maybe this way I would have a greater chance of defeating the deportation order? No; I stopped myself. I needed to stay with my friends and help them. And what of my Shoshana and Gidileh?
> Our boat also advanced towards the *Patria*. We were already very close to the British ship. We could not escape the deportation.

There is a long silence on the cassette and afterwards groans of weeping. That must be Grandma. I turn off the cassette, get up and go out to the garden. My eyes are burning and my head hurts. It's hard for me with everything I've heard, but I am 'grown up'. I rest for a little and hurry back to the cassette player. I'm curious to know what happened. Shoshana, my heroic great-grandmother, continues in a choking voice:

> The British soldiers took hold of me so strongly that my arms were bruised. I held Gidon with all my strength. The waves of the sea soaked the women and children. Shaking from cold we were put on the *Patria*. I could not resist. I didn't want to waste the little strength I had left fighting a lost battle with two men who were stronger than me. I found a place for myself near the stern, held Gidon to me and cried. The tears that had been shut up in me during those three months at sea flowed out and I could not stop them. Even the baby in my arms cried despairingly. I bared a breast. Gidon, wet and shaking, clung to me and nursed avidly. He nursed out all the warmth left in my body. I wrapped him in a rag I found myself sitting on. Tatters of clothing and blankets were scattered all over the ship.
> I was shaking. Suddenly I saw Hanna. She was holding little Rivkaleh in her lap. The little one is blue. I took her from her mother and held her to my breast. She nursed slowly. She was already weary and had no more strength. What now? I looked around me. It was important that I find a place to rest from everything we had gone through.

I found a big bowl, put a rag in it that had been thrown on the floor, put Gidon in the bowl and lay down next to him shaking from cold and fear and waiting for what would come.

This was the longest night of my life. I waited for morning impatiently. I wanted Mittyu with me. The boats continued to come.

Nu, Mittyu, where are you?

23
Prepare for Tomorrow

It is the first light of morning. I decided to get my Gidi ready quickly for what the new day would bring. I changed the rough nappy that was on him for the tatters of an old blanket. The grey clouds had scattered. Jewish and Arab port workers came to the British ship and brought the food ration for the immigrants. The British were 'taking care' that we didn't starve.

I saw one of the porters putting his foot on one of the ladder rungs and tying his shoes. The sack he bore on his back suddenly fell on the coil of rope at one side of the ladder. One of the immigrants went to him and sat down on the same rung of the ladder, waited a few minutes and came quietly back to us. He held a note in his hand, and when he felt surrounded by his friends, opened the note and read in a whisper: 'Start a hunger strike. Don't eat the bread. Only give food to the children. *Prepare for tomorrow.*'

This note had a clear and important message: the Jewish community in the Land was working for the immigrants. The three words at the end – 'prepare for tomorrow' – said everything. Years after that event I read what was written on the note in a document I found in the Illegal Immigration Museum. I was very moved.

A short break. Grandma must've put on glasses to read something.

'Today, Wednesday, 19 Marcheshvan 5701 (20 November 1940), we are starting a general strike of the Jewish community in the land of Israel. We are demonstrating all over the Land and demanding that the entire community stop their work. We will not submit to the evil deportation order. We will not be calm until the immigrants from the three ships step onto the coast of the homeland. We protest before the Mandate government about keeping the immigrants in port, about the lies, about the illegal imprisonment of immigrants in detention camps, about the cruel treatment of Holocaust refugees coming to the Land ill, afraid and hungry. We protest the absence of basic sanitary conditions, about the horrible crowding on the *Atlantic*, the *Milus*, and the *Pacific*, about the abuse of the immigrants and their crowding into the British ship intended for expulsion, about the meagre allowance of water. Be prepared. Signed: Members of the Haganah. Destroy this note.'

This is the note we received on the *Patria*. I am excited to read it after so many years. Everything is coming back to me, as though the things were happening now.

'Prepare for tomorrow', 'Prepare for tomorrow', the rumour spread like wildfire.

What was there to prepare for?

We were still on the hunger strike. My Gidi was asleep. He was exhausted. I felt helpless, weary and hungry. I so wanted one of the portions of bread and fruit that were brought onto the ship, but I knew I must cooperate with the protest of the Jewish community. I waited for Mittyu to join me. I also waited for my sister, her husband and their baby. I waited for Jutyu, who resisted the British soldiers when I was dragged to the boat. Frowning British officers passed between the immigrants and were not impressed by our hunger strike.

'Tomorrow will be a day of order and cleaning on the ship. By eight o'clock in the morning all possessions must be brought on deck,' they announced over the loudspeaker system.

It seems they are preparing the bottom level of the ship to receive the additional refugees that will be brought from the Atlantic, I said to myself. Hundreds of them had not been transferred yet. The *Atlantic* was at least two hundred and fifty metres away.

By evening more boats arrived. Relatives met each other and were moved to tears. My Mittyu was not among them. My eyes were wide open and looking at everyone who was coming on deck: Dinchu? Yosef? Jutyu? No, I didn't see any of them.

Illegal immigrants being transferred to the deportation ship *Patria*

British police patrol everywhere. The wind rose around the ship, and rain poured down, accompanied by lightning and thunder. I was very cold and I could not sleep. Horrible nausea took hold of me. I lifted the bowl Gidon was lying in and prepared to go on deck. Perhaps there I would be eased. Fear and heavy darkness paralyzes me. Suddenly…

Huge thunder shook the *Patria*. The echo of the explosion was so strong that I lost my balance. The alert sirens were heard from every direction. I looked at the sea, it was the refuge for us all. The entire ship shook and water began coming in right where I was standing. The ship leaned to one side. Quickly I took Gidon out of the bowl and held him tightly. With the remainder of my strength I got to the companionway and began climbing. I was not the only one there. Men, women and children pushed each other. I was pushed also. The screams reached to heaven. With one hand I held Gidon to me tightly, and with the other hand I held the rail. The steps were smooth. I lost my balance. The water rose and reached my waist. The hand holding the baby hurt. If only he did not fall from my hand! I was wet and shaking. My legs hardly held me. I tightened my grip on the rail, holding my screaming baby with all my strength, holding tight so that he would not fall from my hands. I pushed forward towards all the others who were climbing the companionway. I was pushed strongly from behind and crushed between everyone else.

I got to the level below the deck. Water had already risen to this place too. The ship listed more and more to one side. A young man who stood next to me took Gidon from me by force. I did not even know who he was. I screamed with all my strength: 'No, no, the child stays with me!' I fought, but the water rose higher and higher. Already it was at my shoulders. I looked for something to hold onto. I looked up. Yes, the porthole above me was open. The man said: '*Nu*, there's no time. Jump. Quickly. Come on! The baby and I will jump after you.'

I was able to take hold of boards and protrusions and climbed up. I was so afraid. To drown after everything we'd gone through? Here, so close to land?

Now, or never. With the little strength I had left I took hold of the window. Someone was pushing me. One shove, and another. I was able to worm through the small window. The water was rising. I had to jump into the water, but I was stuck. I felt strong hands pushing me. I was all scratched – my stomach, back, legs. The blood flowed. I was pricked by rusty nails. I fell into the water head first close to the sinking ship. I was hardly able to lift my head above the water. I breathed a deep breath. The water was frozen. *I must withstand. I must.*

I struggled in the frozen water. Bits of flotsam fell from the ship; boards and parts of the ship floated around me. I moved my hands and legs and tried to breathe. The salt water entered my mouth and my nose. I lost control. I fought to keep my head above the water, to breathe deeply. I choked. I lost my breath. *This is the end.*

Suddenly I felt two brave hands holding me strongly. My saviour had come at the right time. I hear: '*Ma takhfish, ma takhfish* (don't be afraid, don't be afraid).' I didn't understand the words, but I took hold of the 'angel' with all my strength. He swam towards the shore, and I held on tightly. It took us a long time to reach shore, but the strange man brought me to dry land at last.

I lay on the wet sand, frozen and breathless. Only my eyes were wide open and I was looking. I saw people trembling and dishevelled around me. Some of them stepped over me. I slowly rose. Someone wrapped a blanket around me. Two hands lifted me to a nearby lorry. The lorry was loaded with people wailing, shouting, groaning, vomiting. The lorry was on its way.

Going where? Where was my baby? What had happened to those who were left on the *Atlantic*? I cried and called chokingly: 'Gidi, my Gidi, where are you? Mittyu, Mittyu…'

I'd lost the feeling of time and space. The whole way I cried and called the names of those who were dear to me. My cry and shouts were mixed with the commotion around. I was dizzy. I looked for my baby. Where was he? No one could help me. Each one had his own trouble.

The lorry stopped. We were forcibly removed from it and brought to a strange place; a camp with long barracks, surrounded by barbed wire. I was injured, covered in blood and burning salt water. But more than my physical hurt, my heart ached. We were roughly pushed into a big room.

'Disrobe!' we heard an order.

I refused to believe it. What would happen to us?

Now we were all naked. God, *what is happening here?* A sharp smell of DDT choked me. Were we being sprayed? Was it possible? I wanted to run away.

A blanket and some clothes were thrown at me. A queue of women was being led to a long shed. The shed had holes in it. A strong wind blew in. The tin roof moved and creaked as though it would soon fall down on the ones inside. The rain lashed down.

I found a bed. A bed of my own, a privilege. My chest hurt. The time had come to nurse. I felt my chest burning, about to explode. I wanted my baby. Where was he? And where was Mittyu?

In the Atlit detention camp

Still in the camp

24
The Mandate Government Wins Again

Aunt Naama, my mother's sister, has brought me a lot of material about the sinking of the *Patria*. She turned to the archive of the illegal immigrant camp in Atlit and received much material about the event. Naama sits with me. I love to speak with her. She has patience, and she knows how to listen. I always tell her about my thoughts and what I am angry about, but now we talk about the *ha'apala*, the illegal immigration. Only now I start to understand the meaning of this word.

Aunt Naama sits next to me, and we listen to Grandpa Mittyu's voice:

> When what happened had happened I was already on the boat that set out towards the *Patria*. Dinchu, Yosef, baby Yitzhakleh, and my brother Jutyu were also in the boat. On the one hand I was very happy that very soon I would be with my Shoshana and little Gidi, but on the other hand I was pained and insulted about what had been done to us. We yelled vociferously and struck the British soldiers with bitter expressions of anger and frustration. The commotion was great. The waves crashed against the boat and rolled it here and there. The searchlights shone over us and on the raging water. And I, I was planning to jump into the sea. But again I stopped myself. I had to help those who needed me, my sister-in-law and all those in

the boat. I would not abandon them at such a hard hour. We were already very close to the British ship when suddenly we heard a terrible explosion.

We saw the *Patria* sinking. A frightening mountain slowly being swallowed in water. I shouted with all my strength: 'Shoshana! Gidon!' My eyes were filled with salt water and smoke from the explosion. I looked hard – maybe I would see my wife between the raging waves? I saw people jumping from the *Patria*. Shadows of people were being swallowed between the waves and planks were being torn from the ship and falling into the sea. I saw a man moving in the water with a Torah scroll in his hand. Was it not preferable that he would save a child or a baby? I rubbed my eyes and saw splinters of wood, iron, wreckage, hands reaching out from between the waves. Figures were jumping into the water and swimming towards the drowning people. They pulled, towed, stretched out beams of wood. A woman's shouts rent the chaos: 'Where is my child?' And she returned to the sinking ship. I saw a young man swimming with one arm and the water around him was red with blood. Another man and woman tried to lift their heads above the water and disappeared between the waves.

The British soldiers sailed our boat back to the *Atlantic*. More than fifteen hundred frightened immigrants had stayed on the rickety ship, ill and exhausted, disconnected from what was happening and not knowing what the next day would bring.

The worry for my dear ones gave me no rest. What had happened to Shoshana and little Gidileh? Where were they now? Did they survive the explosion? All the immigrants of the *Milus* and the *Pacific* were also on the ship. What had happened to them? The thoughts struck my brain like hammers. I lay on the deck of this filthy ship, my soul speechless from sorrow. If something bad had happened to Shoshana and Gidon I would not be able to live without them. Different thoughts mixed with each other. What had caused the explosion and sinking of the *Patria*?

I don't know how long I lay there, staring. I felt the blood sinking out of me and that I was nothing more than flesh without a soul. Suddenly I heard strange noises in the water close to the ship. I got up from my place and went to the railing. Three men were hanging on the side and with a finger to their lips they stopped me from speaking. Again the people from the Haganah. They came onto the ship. They owed us an explanation.

'A terrible mistake happened. No, we did not mean to sink the *Patria*. Only to bore a small hole in it in order to delay the deportation. We waited for the right time to smuggle the bomb that had been prepared ahead of time in the Technion in Haifa. This was the cleaning day in the ship. The captain of the *Patria* invited technicians from shore to take care of a problem. We saw this as the right time. Immediately we brought Mordechai Meridor, a man of ours from the Haganah. He disguised himself as a port worker, hid the bomb in his mess tin, and gave that to Hans Wendel. He and some more of his friends on the *Patria* took it upon themselves to sabotage the ship. Hans stuck the bomb on the inner side of the ship, and one minute before the explosion he and his friends were able to shout to people to make haste and come on deck immediately. To our sorrow, it became clear that the bomb was too big. A big plank came off the ship, and it began to sink. The ship was old and rickety, and this was not taken into account...'

'Not taken into account? Are you mad?'

He did not answer. The silence between us was thunderous. I shook from anger. I wanted to strangle the men from the Haganah who wanted to prevent the expulsion this way with my bare hands.

'To our sorrow, more than two hundred and fifty people drowned. Now, we will do everything so that you will not be deported. A mistake was made. But ... those who were on the *Patria* and survived the sinking will not be deported. And you, your task is to do all you can. Resist with all your strength.'

The three abandoned us under cover of darkness.

The explosion took place on 25 November 1940, at nine o'clock exactly. It was the hardest day of my life. I stood there for a long time and looked at the water.

We were all helpless, exhausted, frustrated and worried. What had happened to our loved ones? And what of us? Would we be able to overcome the British? We decided to completely disrobe. Maybe shame would prevent them from deporting us?

Many British soldiers were brought to assist in the expulsion. They took us off the ship and loaded us forcibly onto lorries using dogs. We tried to resist. We kicked with our hands and feet, we struck with bats we found and with any item possible. But they overcame us.

The *Patria* explodes and sinks

The lorries were covered with heavy canvas. They threw us some blankets and the lorries set out on their way. We had no idea where we were being taken.

Not long afterwards we were unloaded in a camp where there were some scores of tin barracks. It turned out that the camp was in the city of Akko. We were there for ten days, until we were loaded on trucks again.

Where to this time?

We arrived at the detention camp of Atlit.

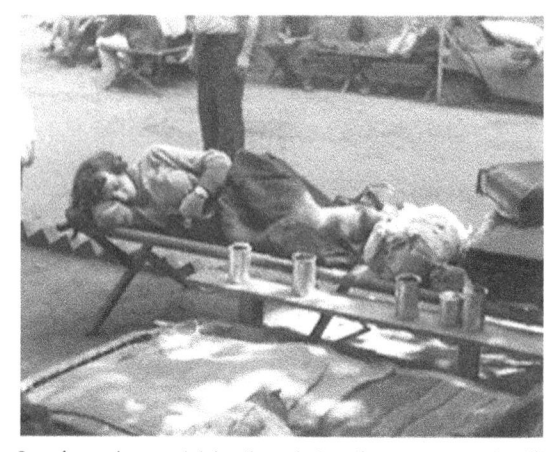

Survivors brought to the detention camp at Atlit

Monument to the Unknown Child and the *Patria* martyrs

25
Rut, and a British Officer

Grandma Reiseleh continues:

I lay dishevelled and injured on the narrow bed. The room was noisy with people. Women walked around, went from bed to bed, everyone was looking… But I had no strength to move. The injuries covering my body became dirty. My chest was heavy, as though lumps of lead had been attached to it. I was shivering continuously. I curled up and wept quietly. A young girl lay in the bed next to mine. She came to me.

'We're neighbours. My name is Rut.'

Tears choked my throat. I succeeded in murmuring only a few words: 'My baby, my husband, my chest hurts.'

The girl drew away from me. What would happen to me?

I lay this way for a long time, until a woman came over to me. She held a baby in her hands.

'Gidileh,' I said with the little strength I had left. I sat up and stretched out my hands to my baby. But no, this was not my Gidileh.

The woman introduced herself: 'I am Bracha. Rut sent me to you. This is my baby, Shloimeleh. I heard your chest hurts. Perhaps, if you would agree to nurse my baby, you will feel better. I have no more milk.'

And before I was able to react, she gave me the baby. I undid the torn blouse I wore, bared a warm, full breast, held the baby next to me, and immediately he began to nurse.

Slowly, slowly the dam of milk opened. He nursed hungrily. His cheek was wet from the abundance of milk. I lifted him up a little so that he would rest. A small boy. Perhaps half a year old. Bigger than my Gidi. One tooth has already grown in his little mouth. I looked at him and cried. Bracha stood next to me. She held out her hands in order to take her Shloimeleh back, but I went on holding him and said: 'One more breast. Please. Shloimeleh is really helping me.'

Again I held him to me next to the left breast. He again started nursing hungrily. The tooth in his mouth crushed my nipple and it pained me, but the nursing helped me very much. When he had finished his mother took him, held him close with her emaciated hands, and said: 'Thank you.'

'Thank you and Shloimeleh. If you like, I'll go on nursing him,' I said.

'And where is your baby?' she asked.

'I don't know. Please, if you hear anything...'

Rut came to me, smiling.

'Do you feel better? Would you like to nurse another baby? We have another baby here.'

I rose from my bed and followed her. At the end of the shed lay a woman, and a baby girl dozed on her chest. No, this is not Hanna, nor is it baby Rivkaleh.

At night I couldn't sleep. Each hour went on for an eternity. My body hurt and my heart longed. I waited for morning to come. Perhaps the new day would bring news and I'd find my baby. The wind struck the tin walls and the rain leaked in again. My bed became completely wet. One drop joined another to become a big puddle between the beds. The girl next to me brought her bed close to mine.

If only morning would come.

Two British officers entered the shed.

'Good morning,' they said, and ordered us all to go to the mess hall.

I rose from the bed. My chest was heavy. The whole room spun around me. I fell on the bed. One of the two officers came and looked at me. For a long time he did not take his eyes off me.

'Why don't you get up?' he asked.

I started to cry. He leaned over, touched my forehead with his hand and went on his way.

I stayed in bed and wept bitterly. The shed emptied. Only I was left lying on the bed, and I felt so very bad. I heard steps drawing near, but I did not move. It was the British officer. He held a tray, with a cup of tea and two biscuits.

'Drink,' he said to me. 'Drink!'

I drank the tea thirstily. The biscuits stayed on the tray. I was so very thirsty.

'What is your name?' he asked.

'Reiseleh, Shoshana.'

'And the family name?'

'Grinfeld. Grinfeld.'

I looked at the officer standing next to me. Maybe he would be my saving angel?

'Perhaps you know something about my baby? About my husband? About Gidon Grinfeld, about Mittyu Grinfeld?' I asked and burst into tears again. 'Please, please, I need your help,' I said to him in his own language and tears choked my throat.

Again he looked at me for a long time, and left without saying a word. I stayed sitting, helpless. My questions were left without an answer.

The women came back from the mess hall. Rut came back to the shed and gave me a carafe full of tea. I quickly swallowed it all and went back to staring at the ceiling. I became feverish again and my chest was very painful. Shloimeleh's mother was afraid to let me nurse him. Perhaps I had malaria? Perhaps typhus?

I sat up to extract some milk from my chest with pressure, but not one drop came out. I continued to press. I thought my chest would burst. The milk stayed sealed inside. It must have turned to cheese. The fever continued to rise. I began to hallucinate.

That afternoon the camp doctor, also a British officer, arrived. He looked at me with apathetic eyes and gave me a cursory examination. *They have not one small trace of humanity,* I thought to myself. He seemed distant, as though I were not a survivor who had almost lost her life. He did not ask questions, but only took two pills out of the bag he had brought with him.

'Swallow them,' he said.

I swallowed. I would have swallowed a frog, if only it would stop the pain. He did not explain what the pills were for, and I did not ask. After I swallowed he continued without a word. He went to a girl who burned with fever in a bed far away from me.

I fell asleep. I slept for a long time. When I opened my eyes I felt that the pressure in my chest had lessened, but the lead weights were still heavy and bothersome. I must take myself in hand. I must be my own doctor. Enough crying. Enough groaning. I must gather together all the strength I had in order to go on and find Mittyu and Gidi. I tried to sit. It was an impossible task. With my first attempt to rise I reeled with dizziness; the roof above my head looked as though it were dancing, and a sick fog blinded my eyes. My head was heavy. I lay back down. I waited for a few minutes and again tried to sit. I sat for a short time. I did not dare to stand.

For two more days I burned with fever. The milk in my breasts gradually lessened. I recovered a little. I felt someone putting cold cloths on my forehead. When I opened my eyes I saw Rut. Such a young girl, maybe fourteen, not more. She poured sweet, lukewarm tea into my mouth and then stroked my head. I smiled to her, and she answered me with a sad smile.

Rut did not know what had happened to her parents and her younger brother. She had looked everywhere and could not find any of them. I asked if she heard about other survivors from the *Patria*. No, she had not heard anything. She could only tell me that some two hundred and fifty victims had been taken from the ship, two mothers and two babies among them. Those who had survived had been brought here.

'I heard that the one who saved the situation was a young British Navy officer,' she told me. 'The officer pushed between the crowds gathered on the deck and ran to the steam boilers in the engine room. There he released the steam cocks and prevented the ship from exploding together with everyone in it and around it. There, by the boilers, they found his body.'

'And where are the men?'

'The men? They have been put in separate sheds. Rabbi Tannenbaum was also saved from the explosion. They say that he succeeded in getting to shore with a Torah scroll.'

'And how did you get to shore?' I asked.

'I jumped into the water. It's lucky I know how to swim. A huge pool of blood gathered around me. I swam in a sea of blood. A barrel rolled near me and injured my arm. The pain was terrible, but I took hold of the barrel with my left hand because I had no more strength left to swim. A huge wave covered me and swept the barrel away. I swam towards it with one arm and managed to get to it. I took hold of the handle first and then a plank of wood that floated on the water next to me. I wanted to lie on it to rest for a little, but the waves again covered me. Luckily, an Arab fisherman saw me, swam towards me, tied the plank with the rope that he had and towed me to shore. The whole way he called to me: '*Ma takhfish, ma takhfish.*' He put me on the sand and went back into the sea. I saw him swimming towards people who were waving their hands. So far I haven't found anyone, neither my brother nor my parents. I have been looking for them for seven days, since the explosion.'

26
A Bitter Day

Grandpa Mittyu begins to speak:

We had reached the detention camp at Atlit. My brother-in-law, Yosef, is with me. Dinchu and Yitzhakleh have been moved to another shed. Again we are separated. Perhaps I will find my Reiseleh here? It was winter, and the cold penetrated deep into our bones. For ten days we were incarcerated in the long sheds allotted to us. We were not permitted to go out and we could not find out who else was here. British policeman in uniform surrounded our shed.

On the eleventh day, early in the morning, at exactly 06:20, we heard a commotion around the sheds. Through the narrow windows we saw thousands of soldiers surrounding the structure and with them were officials in civilian dress. I saw armoured cars on the surrounding hills, their mounted rifles trained on us. We heard barking dogs. Apparently they wanted to prevent us from any attempt at escape or responding with force.

We all, without prior consultation, undressed and lay down on the floor. If we needed to, we would resist the British plans with force. We heard cries of women and children from neighbouring sheds. Shouts and curses accompanied the sounds of weeping. Among them we could clearly hear the voice of Saunders, the well-known British police inspector: '*Attack!*' he shouted.

All those who were ordered to, stormed the sheds. There were three British soldiers for every immigrant. We kicked them and used our hands to strike with all of our meagre strength. We took hold of the iron beds in order to resist. The floor was covered with blood. The wounded lay on it and cried in pain. Even the strong wind came in and joined the chorus of wails. The tin roof rattled, the doors creaked and were slammed to their lintels, and the dogs attacked us with bared teeth.

I was taken away through the women's shed. I saw many of them struggling with all their strength, taking hold of whatever they could, striking with their fists. The policemen raged. Breathless, they cursed us. I heard one of the women shouting: 'Even in Buchenwald they did not treat us like this!'

The blanket that was put on me was covered with blood. The smell of perspiration and blood filled the air. Two policemen left the scene and returned the way they had come. It was hard to believe that they did this because of physical weakness. Perhaps they were ashamed of their deeds?

One of our young men fainted. The woman next to him shouted and cursed in German. The policemen used the batons to strike to the left and the right. They hit my head. I lost my balance and fell. Policemen fell on me from every side, and I was able to kick with my feet and ball my hands into fists in order to strike, but they were stronger than I and struck all parts of my body without mercy. I lost all feeling. I only felt that I was being dragged, lifted and thrown into a lorry.

Our struggle lasted eight hours. We had no strength for more than that.

We were crowded into a lorry, pale, shivering with cold and covered with blood and sweat, and the canvas was closed over us.

It was quiet now. Silent. Each one of the people in the lorry was sunk deep inside themselves, their head between their knees. The crunch of lorry wheels overcame the sound of choked weeping. Suddenly I saw Dinchu sitting opposite me. She embraced her Yitzhakleh with her wounded hands. Her blue eyes were dark with fury. A deep cut in her neck bled heavily. I tore a piece off my blanket and gave it to her so that she could wrap it around her neck and stop the bleeding.

She wept. I also wept with her.

We got to Haifa. It was 9 December. A horrible, bitter day. We were forcibly put on a Dutch ship. Another ship was anchored nearby. More than seventeen hundred immigrants to be deported were put on the two ships.

We were naked and exhausted. Insult and fury filled my entire being. So this was 'justice'?

27
Bilhah, My Angel

I continue to investigate. Grandma Aliza joins my search. She tries very much to help.

'Grandma Reiseleh had friends in the kibbutz Givat HaShloshah who helped her very much during her first days in the country. I am sure that Bilhah Kaminer will be able to shed light of her own on your great-grandmother's immigration story,' she suggested.

I jump at the idea. Within a few days we get organized and go to visit her at Givat HaShloshah. She's already more than eighty-five, but she is still coherent and remembers everything. She's happy to meet with me. I tell her about the work I'm doing, and that I have many details missing about my grandmother's immigration story and her first days in Israel. I ask if she still remembers.

Bilhah gives me a heartfelt smile.

'*Nu*, how could I forget? I remember the letters I received from some of our friends from the "Young Pioneers" very well. They wrote that they were together with Mittyu and Reiseleh in the camp in Bratislava, waiting to board a ship for Israel, and they wrote even that the two of them had a sweet baby, and that they were worried how he would survive the immigration.'

'What else do you know about them? Tell me.'

'When we heard that the *Patria* exploded and that 250 people had died, I told my husband, Chaim, that I must go to Atlit. I was sure that some of our friends from the "Young Pioneers" were in the detention camp and I wanted to help.

'I reached Atlit on 30 November 1940. I stood at the camp's gate and asked one of the guards there for permission to go in and visit my friends. He sent someone to ask the commander if this is possible. I waited in the severe cold for two hours. I curled up in my coat and held the heavy bag I had filled with good things: biscuits I had baked, oranges from the kibbutz's orchard, and other good food. I missed my friends. I knew they had gone through many troubles.

'Close to noon the soldier came back and said: "OK." Before he opened the gate for me he wanted to check the contents of my bag. I gave him an orange to thank him. He smiled and directed me to the women's shed. I asked one of them if there were women there who had come from Bratislava. Immediately she pointed towards a bed in the corner of the shed and said: "She's lying there, ill."

'Reiseleh slept on a narrow, stinking bed. Her cheeks were flushed. I touched her forehead. She burned from fever. When she felt the touch, she opened her eyes. They were deep as two blue wells with all the pain of the world gathered inside them.

'"Reiseleh, Reiseleh, how are you?'

'Reiseleh stretched her emaciated hands towards me. "Bilhah, Bilhah Kaminer. How did you get here?"

'Before I was able to answer her, she started to cry. I stroked her head and tried to calm her. My tears fell on her hair. *What does she look like? Where are the sparkling eyes I knew? Where is the captivating smile?*

'I peeled an orange for her. She licked the juice thirstily. Her lips were dry. "Bilhah, it's so good to see you. How are you?"

"'I'm all right. Chaim is well too. Our Yiftach is growing well. How are you?"

Again she burst into tears.

"'Why are you crying? You're here in Israel at last. Everything will be well."

"'Bilhah, I don't know where my baby is. I don't know what happened to Mittyu."

'I helped Shoshana to sit and sat down next to her. Shoshana told me weakly how they had almost drowned but at the last minute someone took the baby out of her hands without asking her permission.

"'Everything happened so quickly. I could not resist. The water already overflowed the ship, and it was about to sink. I argued with him for one second, but the water had already got to my shoulders, and I had no choice. I feel guilty, as though I abandoned him."

'I told Shoshana what I knew from the newspapers and radio. I knew that whoever had remained on the *Atlantic* had been exiled to Mauritius.

"'Where is Mauritius?" she asked.

"'Reiseleh, Mauritius is an island in the Indian Ocean. The British incarcerated many of the immigrants in the detention camp there. Write there," I suggested to her. "Maybe one of the letters will reach its goal. Maybe they will answer you."

"'Dear Bilhah, thank you. You were always my angel. I will write today. I will write to Mittyu, to my brother-in-law, Yosef, and my sister, Dinchu, and I will also write to Jutyu. By the way, my name isn't Reiseleh anymore. My name is Shoshana."

'A young British officer entered and approached Shoshana's bed. He looked at her and smiled. I looked at him. For some reason he did not look British to me. He had a captivating smile. In one hand he held a suitcase. When he approached us he lifted it and asked Shoshana if it was hers.

'She burst into heartrending tears. She stretched out her hands for the old brown suitcase, the one marked with the name "Grinfeld", held it to her and said: "Yes, thank you. This was the suitcase that was with me on the exploded ship. Perhaps you know something about my baby? If the suitcase was found, maybe…? Please, please…"

"'Mrs Grinfeld, there are survivors from the *Patria* in the hospitals. Adults, young people and babies too. If you like, in two days I will have a jeep, I can take you to Haifa. We will go through the hospitals, and maybe there…"

'Shoshana held the British soldier's hand between both of hers to show him how grateful she was.

"'Thank you, thank you from the bottom of my heart. On Thursday morning I will be waiting for you."

'I found Shoshana a blue dress with long sleeves from a pile of clothes that had been thrown on the floor. I combed her dishevelled hair. She had golden hair, but now it was sticky from the salt it had absorbed.

"'Shoshana, you must shower," I said.

'She smiled at me, and the light shone again from her beautiful face.

'I left my whole parcel with Shoshana. I did not have the time to look for other acquaintances in the camp. The next time I came, Shoshana would probably know more about Mittyu and her baby, and then I would be able to look for my friends. Maybe I would find them.

'I went back to the kibbutz, sad. The things I had seen did not leave me. How was it possible to treat people this way, who suffered so much? How could cultured people imprison others in a detention camp, surrounded by barbed wire in unacceptable conditions? How much longer would they keep them there?'

Bilhah sighs. From her face I can see that she's weary. She looks at us apologetically and says: 'I'm a little tired. I'll be happy if you come and visit me again. So maybe next week?'

We return home. I wait impatiently for the mystery of the lost baby to be solved.

28
Mauritius

Grandpa Mittyu is speaking:

Again we were sailing. This time under heavy police escort. We had been forcibly put onto two Dutch ships. In our ship everyone was sitting silent, but the silence was thunderous. We'd come to a decision: they would not break us. We would stay unified and, with unified strength, find a way to overcome all the evil edicts against us. We would go back to Israel at any price and in any possible way, in spite of them. We would build our country, or homeland, in spite of everything. This was our goal, and all means were permitted. One of the people sitting opposite me muttered a prayer. Each to his own faith…

We returned to the roll and toss of the sea. Again the vomiting, the hunger and the illness, as though what we had gone through on the *Atlantic* was not enough. For three weeks we were tossed towards an unknown destination. The humidity was high, and we were always wet with perspiration. It was clear that we were sailing south. We surmised this according to the location of the sunrise and the sunset. Judging by the intolerable humidity, it seemed that we were on the equator.

'Perhaps we are sailing in the Indian Ocean,' someone suggested.

A typhus epidemic spread in the ships. Three people died. As was customary, they were thrown overboard after a short prayer. Their struggle had ended. They would rest, at peace between the waves, and we would draw new strength from their death. Their death would become a driving force. The burgeoning fury spurred us on in the struggle... But after a few days I lost not only the sense of time, but also the sense of vengeance. I stopped hoping. I felt the burning seeping out.

'We have reached the island of Mauritius,' the ship's captain announced.

We were permitted to disembark from the ships. We were surprised to find a busy port. A train moved on its tracks, buses waited at bus stops, taxis, cars, passers-by in colourful clothes, storefronts filled with goods, venders hawking their wares. Life.

We were led to a camp surrounded by high walls with guard towers. It seemed that the island was well guarded by the local British police. There was no way to escape from here.

There was pouring rain, and the air was hot and stifling. The environs of the camp were swamps filled with mosquitoes. We heard that malaria governed the island. I was exhausted. I dozed and hallucinated more than I was awake. I saw Shoshana smiling at me, and I felt the weight of my Gidi on my chest. I felt good with these hallucinations.

The men were separated from the women and children, and we were led to two stone structures. We soon found that this was the Beau-Bassin jail. It was surrounded by a five-metre high wall, and sentries stood at the gates watching over the comings and goings twenty-four hours a day.

The cells in these two big buildings were dreadfully narrow. There were three storeys. I was put in the middle storey, in a cell that was about three metres long and about a metre or a metre and a quarter wide. Canvas was stretched in the cell to serve as beds. Jutyu and Yosef were put in the same row, not far away from my own cell.

The women were taken to long structures made of tin. I felt sorry for them. I knew very well that there was nothing like tin to warm you in the summer and cool you in the winter. From far away we heard the thunder of the roofs rattling in the wind and wanting to blow away. This noise must be keeping the children from falling asleep. I was worried about Dinchu and Yitzhakleh. Here and there we saw bits of roofs being blown away. The fear was terrible. It was miraculous that none of them were injured.

When storms like this began we would run terrified into the building, protecting our heads with our arms to fend off any falling piece of tin.

One of the guards told me that the cyclone was on the way and we must prepare. We tied down everything that was likely to be blown away in the wind, strengthened the windows and tied down the little bit of furniture securely. A whirlwind of dust and sand told of the coming of the cyclone, and afterwards the entire compound was filled with dust devils. Entire structures were blown from their place.

When at last the storm was over we went out to see what it had done – and the entire surroundings were painted a dusty grey. Not one green leaf was to be seen in the covering of dust. I met Yosef outside. 'Since we came I have not seen Dinchu and Yitzhakleh,' he said.

The men were forbidden from seeing their wives and children, and all the protests were of no use. The conflicts with the prison guards grew more common. It was hard for them to withstand our anger. 'We did not invent the laws,' they said. 'We are simply following orders from above.' In spite of these explanations the arguments did not stop. We found out that the soldiers around us were helpless, and this increased the pressure we put on them.

A few weeks later the British grew a little more lax and lightened the restrictions. They allowed the men to meet with the women, but twice a week and for a few hours only.

Yosef waited impatiently for the day when he could see Dinchu and the child. He came back to our structure, his face shining, after having visited them.

'Yitzhakleh is growing nicely. He is already starting to speak, but I'm not happy that he mumbles words in German,' he said.

'Most of the women in the shack are refugees from Germany. They all speak German, apparently,' I tried to supply a logical explanation.

I have forged a connection with a native policeman. He is the one who told me the camp we were staying in served in the past as a jail, and had been built by the French many years before. He also told me about the war and about the German army which was moving swiftly towards North Africa on its way to the land of Israel. I also learned from him that the British army desperately needed reinforcements, and the Czech army as well, which was fighting against the Nazis alongside the Allies.

Grandpa's voice sounds faint, and right afterwards a long silence falls. Grandpa clears his throat and asks to stop at this point. He's tired, and wants to drink something hot.

How can someone not be tired from memories like these? Aunt Naama and I look at each other. I see the moisture in her eyes, as she must've seen in mine.

'You know, Roni, the fact that we are here in our country, and the fact that you have a wonderful home and family, and the fact you are looking for your roots, is our grandparents' great victory.'

We both laugh through the tears. Naama's eyes are shining.

'Nemi,' I say, 'it must be very hard for Grandpa to tell his story. The memories from that hard time exhaust him. The longing and the worry for his family were impossible to bear. What happened to them? Are they alive? I am sure that these questions gave him no rest.'

Naama gets up from her place. She brings a carafe of cold water, pours a glass for herself and for me and we drink quietly, together with the grandparents.

Arriving at the detention camp in Mauritius: the illegal immigrants waving the flag and singing: "Our hope is not yet lost…"

In the jail at Mauritius

29
Malaria, and a Letter

I show my aunt Naama my paper. She pages through it, and as she does so she strokes my hair and smiles. Naama has many memories of Grandpa Mittyu and Grandma Reiseleh. I see that she is very excited.

'Do you have an atlas?' she asks.

I bring the atlas and put it on my knees. We both look for the island of Mauritius. We see the string of islands in the Indian Ocean, and sail with our finger from the ocean to Israel.

'How would Mittyu be able to escape this jail? Will he have to wait until they change the White Paper laws? This isn't a white paper, it's a black paper. Who is the criminal, the one who enforces obedience to a draconian law, or the one who breaks it? Is the "criminal" the one who has no place in the world to live except here, and he wants to come here, or the one who prevents him?'

I ask many other questions: Where was the world? Where were the good people? Why did they not lift a finger to help? More than expecting an answer, I want to unload the tension.

My mother has come home. The three of us sit together and talk. We have gathered together a load of questions that have no answers.

Ima tries to supply an explanation: 'This war trampled all human emotion. The world lost its sanity. There was complete chaos. Everyone was against everyone, and in all this horrible commotion the Jews were butchered. Those who did succeed in escaping, no country agreed to receive. Each country acted according to its own interests with their eyes closed and their heart sealed against the pain of an entire people.'

Nu, and I need to calm down after an explanation like this?

Two more days pass before I can return to the cassette. The answer that Ima gave pecks at my mind, but more than that pecks the answerless questions.

Grandpa begins to speak again.

The heat and the humidity on Mauritius wreaked havoc on us. The women would go out with the children under the coconut and mango trees to enjoy a little bit of coolness. The tin shack blazed with heat. We ate mangoes, coconuts and bananas for every meal, day in, day out.

Dinchu came to see Yosef and was holding Yitzhakleh in her arms. They saw each other only at certain times and only twice a week.

'Dina, have you heard something?'

'No. Nothing. The women chat. Some of them also received letters. I listen and ask, but no, there is no news.'

I played with Yitzhakleh. Every contact with the baby brought back my desire to continue living, to continue searching.

The days went by slowly. Lazily. We had to lead as 'normal' a life as possible here. We must not fall into despair. Action was the best medicine. Everyone did what he knew how to do.

At first I worked in construction. I repaired cracks, painted, repaired a door here and a window there. Afterwards I went to work in a shoemaker's shop. I repaired the shoes of the internees in the camp. Yosef roasted coffee and ground it. There were many craftsmen among us. Each one contributed from his own knowledge and abilities. The women taught and sewed. They made a sewing workshop, and the men organized a shoemaker's, blacksmith's, carpenter's, and even an industry. We made brushes, knick-knacks and toys. We used material that was abundant on the island – agave leaves and roots, coconut rinds, bark of trees, shells – we used all these to make tools, decorations and toys. There was no end to our imagination. We opened a store in the camp and 'sold' what we had made with our own hands. The paper industry flourished as well. We made paper from the agave bushes. When the production increased over our demand, we began to export outside the island. The local markets bought everything we offered, and the hawkers pounced on the merchandise we brought. The money was gathered into a common fund, we appointed a treasurer who would take care of the money and use it to purchase everything that was necessary for the good of the community. We lived a communal life.

The British sent some of our men to work outside the camp in British army workshops. Some of us were vehicle mechanics, others were engineers and maintenance workers, and others were farmers. The land gave a good harvest for the welfare of us all.

An abundance of paper meant that we were able to correspond with whoever we could think of, in order to understand what was going on outside our jail. Some friends from the 'Young Pioneers' were with me, and we continued with the Zionist activity. We tried to find out what had happened to the friends who were on the *Patria* but no news about this reached us.

We founded a school. Dinchu taught there too. The Bishop of Mauritius helped as well, and contributed school books for us. We published a weekly newspaper. We gathered the news from listening to the radio, chiefly the local station, and from the newspaper we received in the camp. It was important for us to keep alert and to be informed. We also had an orchestra. We had a pianist, an accordionist, a drummer and two violinists. The orchestra played at festive occasions, and on the Jewish holidays the teachers would invite it to play songs at the school. Among other skills, the children learned drawing and sculpting, and at the end of the year they displayed their works in an exhibition.

But the heat and humidity exhausted us all. Sometimes the heat reached 50°C, and together with the humidity acted against us. Typhus, fever and even polio spread in the camp and began to claim victims. One of the most beautiful little girls in the camp grew sick and died a few days later. Fifty-four of our members fell ill and did not rise again. We buried them in the ground we had dedicated as a graveyard, there in a foreign land.

Winter approached. Cyclones again threatened the island. We had learned how to predict the coming of the storm. It always began with a little innocent cloud sailing apathetically in the sky, growing and growing until it became a monster. With the first signs we all participated in security measures: sealing windows, tying down roofs and anything that was likely to blow away in the destructive wind.

The first cyclone storm that winter began at night: pouring rain came down on the camp accompanied by increasingly noisy wind. We heard heavy thumps. Roofs came off the women's sheds and sheets of tin were torn away from their place. Yosef was worried for Dina and Yitzhakleh. He stayed at the entrance to the building and waited to see what would happen. I stood next to him. Wind whipped our faces. Women wrapped in coats and headscarves carried the little children in their arms, and pulled the bigger ones quickly to our stone building. Dinchu came also. She and Yitzhakleh were completely soaked. We brought the women in to our small cells to stay until the storm passed.

Then came hard news from outside.

In Europe the Jews were being led to extermination camps: they were being destroyed in crematoriums, in killing ditches, and even in gas chambers. The Germans were making the method more efficient in order to hurry and reach a decisive and 'Final Solution'. The gas chambers were working ceaselessly. Tens of thousands of Jews choked to death in them. Jews from all over the conquered lands were brought in cattle cars to Auschwitz, Treblinka, Dachau, Bergen-Belsen, every hour. We heard that Ben-Gurion, the premier in Israel, received the horrible reports from two survivors who escaped Auschwitz. He immediately sent messengers to

London and to the United States. He was demanding the world's intervention: 'The destruction of our people must stop at once,' he said.

Messengers from the Land went out to the ends of the earth, and were treated as a nuisance everywhere. They were dismissed with 'go' and 'return'... 'Yes, we are taking care of this...'

Ben-Gurion demanded that the Allies bomb Auschwitz, even if it meant the death of all who were in the camp. But sometime afterwards he changed his mind. He feared for the hundreds of thousands of refugees there. It seemed that even the world powers fighting the Nazis battled this question of whether they should bomb the camps or not.

News had also reached us about what was happening on the coasts of the Land. We heard about other immigrant ships – more people deported.

God in heaven, your chosen people are being destroyed in camps in Europe; here in the Promised Land they're not being allowed onto the shore that will save them. And you sit there and are silent?

During the night I awoke drenched in sweat. I was completely wet and a horrible shudder took hold of me. I shivered and my teeth chattered. After a wave of cold struck me a wave of heat came. I breathed slowly, and tried to calm down. For a week I lay delirious. Yosef and Jutyu took care of me devotedly. Yosef summoned his doctor friend who had been with us on the *Atlantic*. The doctor gave me medicine, but I had no strength to swallow it. Yosef sat next to me and with great patience wiped away the sweat on my face, put cold cloths on my forehead, crumbled the pills, mixed the dust with a sweet tea and gave it to me to drink. Slowly, slowly the fever was brought down. Yosef fed me with a bit of soup Dina had cooked for me, spoonful after spoonful. The smell of the soup reminded me of home in Ungvar. Ima made a soup like this.

In delirium I repeatedly asked, 'Where is Shoshana? Where is Gidon?'

For many days I lay exhausted, apathetic to everything around me. Jutyu, my brother, sat next to me for many long hours. He took care of everything I needed.

My friends urged me to return to work. They said that it would bring me back to a routine. I returned, but my mood stayed as depressed as it had been. I was consumed with longing and worry.

One day, my brother came to the shoemaker's shop, excited.

'Mittyu, Mittyu, you have a letter. You have a letter!'

I opened the envelope with trembling hands, and my eyes filled with tears. I immediately recognized my Reiseleh's beautiful, orderly handwriting. I could not read. The letters danced before my eyes.

30
Good Siblings and Uncle Yoav

Shiri, my sister, looks at me and asks: 'Roni, why are you crying?'

I do not answer. I only wipe away the tears.

'Gosh, it must be because of this "roots" project. Just write about Ima and Abba. What do you need all this research for? You're a fool. Tell your teacher that you won't…'

I stop Shiri in the middle of her sentence. 'Even if they exempt me from writing the paper,' I said, 'I won't stop. When you have to write a paper like this yourself, you'll understand.'

Shiri laughs: 'What, am I a tree that I need roots?'

Even though Shiri is too young to understand, it could be that she is right. Maybe I have dug too deep; I've reached roots that are too deep. So many questions fill my mind. And Grandpa Gidi does not answer them for me. I sometimes feel like a detective following hidden secrets. Uncle Yoav calls and promises to bring me more material. He was Great-grandfather and Great-grandmother's first grandchild, and he heard many stories from them.

The sun is already wrapped in her pink bedclothes when I go with Shiri into the garden. Rotem, my brother, gives me a plastic bag.

'That's for you,' he says. 'I want to help you with the paper you're doing.'

I open the bag and find weeds he has pulled up from the garden in it.

'What's this?' I say.

'Roots,' he says. 'I brought them for you for your paper. You can glue them in your notebook.'

I laugh heartily. My little brother is so cute. Shiri and I run to the trampoline in the yard, and little Tali joins us. The three of us get on it and jump. When we get tired we go and eat the bananas and oranges that Grandpa Gidi brought for us. I love the orange season when our garden blossoms with so many colours. Gold, purple and crimson pansies flower together with narcissus. The grass is green, and the tops of the trees shine from the light rain that just fell. A clean smell fills the air.

'Shiri, I'm going back to work. Watch over Tali.'

'Roots, roots,' she laughs at me. 'If they give me this punishment too, I'll take a hoe and shovel and start digging…' And immediately I hear her laughing a laugh full of joy.

Such is Shiri my sister. I call her 'funny face'. She always has a joke, or something witty to say. She's the best.

We talk a lot in class about what the children have learned about their families. There are many stories about the heroism of their grandparents in every corner of the world. Each one of the children has a story of war, starvation, suffering, death, and also about *aliyah*, settlement and heroism. The teacher uses the word 'resurrection' a lot when we talk about our people who conquered the bereavement, pain and suffering, and rose up like a phoenix. And now we must defend everything we have. Nothing here can be taken for granted.

I'm starting to understand my father, who serves in the army. He leaves home early, comes back after we're already asleep, and sometimes even stays at work at night. And my uncle Yoav too. Many times I have been angry that Abba has not dedicated time for us, and that he's not at home at all.

'I'm continuing from where my grandparents left off,' he says to me again and again – and this must explain everything.

Again I'm at the cassette player. Grandpa Mittyu continues with his story.

> I hold Reiseleh's letter and my hands are trembling from excitement. There are many stamps on the envelope. The letter must have travelled a long way until it got to me. It was written about two weeks after the sinking of the *Patria*, and only now has reached me. I read slowly, slowly, drinking each word thirstily, trying to understand...
>
> 4 December 1941
>
> My dear Mittyu,
> I hope this letter will reach you. Bilhah Kaminer came to visit me here, at Atlit, and I heard from her that whoever stayed on the *Atlantic* was deported to the island of Mauritius in the Indian Ocean.
> As you will see, I survived! His Majesty's government pardoned all the immigrants who were on the Patria, and moved us to At...
>
> I turned over the paper. It was hard for me to understand what was written on it. The ink was smudged. *I must know what happened to our Gidi.* The paper was silent and the letters were erased. I could not decipher them. Shoshana was in the Atlit internment camp. And I was there too for ten days before we were deported...

Grandpa's voice was cut off exactly at this point. I press the 'play' button again and again, but the cassette is not working. I take it out. The audio ribbon has got stuck. This is all I need! I hope that we'll be able fix it before it's ruined. Ima and Abba are not at home, but I must continue and listen. Right at the most gripping moment of the cassette the ribbon decided to get twisted!

Shiri has come back from jazz class. Tali hugs her. Rotem has come home with a friend. I go to Shiri and hug her. 'I'm so glad I have you.'

Rotem runs to me. He also gets a hug and a kiss. He hurries to be with his friend in order to repair the bicycle that he received not long ago.

Shiri looks at me with her big sea-blue eyes and asks, '*Nu*, what's going on?'

'I'm frustrated. There's a problem. The tape in the cassette has got stuck.'

'That's great. You'll be able to finish this paper of yours at last, and have more time for me.'

'Did you know that Grandma Reiseleh was saved after the ship she was on exploded? And now I don't know what happened to her baby.'

'What don't you know? Grandpa Gidi is Gidon. He was her child. So he must've been saved.'

Nu, I think to myself. Shiri's got good logic. But it's not so simple. Maybe Gidi, who is Gidon my grandfather, is not the baby who was saved? Perhaps he is another baby who was born to Reiseleh? I share my thoughts with Shiri.

'What's the problem?' she answers right away. 'We'll just ask Grandpa Gidi, and that's it.'

Everything is always simple for Shiri. Everything is much more complicated for me.

'And if Grandpa won't tell? Maybe he himself doesn't know the truth? Perhaps he doesn't want to tell? I've already asked him all sorts of questions, and he is very evasive. He has secrets he doesn't want to reveal.'

'I'm going to call him. I'll just call him, and that's it.'

'Shiri, one second. I have an idea. The *Patria* sank on 25 November 1940, and the baby was almost a month old when he came with Grandma and Grandpa on the *Atlantic*. So according to my calculation, the baby was a little bit more than three months old when he came to the Land. So…'

'What, you think a three-month-old baby will remember something? Roni, you're really funny.'

'Silly. You don't understand where I'm going. If Grandpa Gidi is the baby who was on the *Patria* when it exploded, that means he was born in 1940. Right? So all I need to know is what year Grandpa Gidi was born. We'll ask him when his birthday is. What do you think?'

'Wow, Roni, I didn't know you were so clever. A real detective…'

We both go to the phone. I asked Shiri to talk to Grandpa. I suggest that she talks about birthdays, like her birthday that will be coming up soon, and nonchalantly ask about birthdays of family members, and his also… Shiri dials. We wait for an answer. The phone rings and rings, and in the end we reach the voicemail. Grandpa Gidi is not at home.

Right then Ima came in. I run to her, hug her and say: 'Ima, the ribbon in the cassette has stuck. Do you think we can repair it and go on listening?'

Shiri comes over. 'Ima, I was born on 9 March, right, and you and Abba in May, and Grandpa Gidi in… *Nu*, Ima, I forget. What year was Grandpa born? What month?'

Rotem is crying. He's fallen down and hurt his knee badly. It's bleeding. Ima goes to him and hugs him. Now she's busy. She washes Rotem's knee in the shower. Shiri goes on.

'Come on, Ima, you didn't tell me.'

'Shiri, don't you see your brother's hurt? Don't you see I'm busy now? Do me a favour, calm Tali down.' While she's taking care of Rotem, Ima tries to do that: 'Tali, don't cry. Rotem's knee doesn't hurt so much. See, he's fine.'

When the house calms down a little, and Ima at last sits down to rest, I give her a glass of water to drink and sit next to her. I see she is very tired. She has had a long work day, Abba won't come home tonight, and she doesn't have much patience for questions. I want to make her happy.

'Tonight Shiri and I, and Rotem and Tali too, will make supper. You're our guest. We'll spoil you,' I say. Shiri and I now stand in the kitchen and whisper to each other. Ima tidies up the house. There are letters on the table. She checks the paperwork, puts a load of laundry in the machine, runs outside and brings the dry laundry in. We'll help her fold it. We love Ima, and it's important that we protect her.

When we finish eating, I wash the dishes. From there I go straight into the shower, and now we are all in pyjamas. At last Rotem and Tali have fallen asleep. This is the time.

'Ima, how do I go on? The cassette stuck right when Grandma was telling how she was saved from drowning on the ship that exploded. And what about the baby?'

There's a knock on the door. I open it and see Uncle Yoav. He smiles at me and lifts me very high. When my feet are on the floor again he asks me: 'So, how are your roots?'

Shiri runs to him too. She also wants a hug. Yoav takes out some lollipops. He gives one to Shiri and two more that we should keep for Rotem and Tali.

'What about me?' I ask.

'I brought something for you too.' He takes a computer disk out of his shirt pocket.

'Yoav, I don't have time for computer games. I must finish my paper. Give the disk to Shiri, she'll be glad for a few more games.'

'Roni, this is for you. I brought it from the Illegal Immigration Museum in Haifa. I sat there for a long time and looked for material. There is material here about the illegal immigration, about the Atlantic, about the Patria and also about Mauritius.'

I hug my dear uncle. Even though he's in the army, and he has no spare time, and hardly sees Mia, his wife, and Yahli, Idan and Gilad, my cousins, he still went especially to Haifa, invested time and energy, and brought me a disk…

'Yoavi, I love you so much. As you're already here, maybe you can help me with another small thing? The cassette tape is stuck. The ribbon has got twisted, and Abba isn't here yet.'

I know Uncle Yoav is in a hurry. He wants to be able to see Mia and the children, but he still sits down by the cassette player. He takes the cassette and turns it around gently to release the ribbon, rolls it slowly onto the spool, and the ribbon is in place. We only need to check. He puts the cassette into the player.

'Everything is OK, Roni.'

Yoav takes leave of each one of us with a hug and a kiss, and in a few minutes we hear his jeep driving away. He's going home. How good it is that I have uncles like this.

I won't listen to the cassette today any more. It's too late. Before we go to sleep I tell Shiri that I actually want to wait. Not knowing is making me more and more curious. It's not bad at all to be in suspense. It adds spice to life. Shiri agrees with me.

'You know that I love challenges,' she says, 'and I also have more patience than you. It's not at all the thing to get all the answers at once. All the fun is in finding things out slowly. It's good that you know how to dig deep and find treasures. I've also got this "bug". I think we'll both be archaeologists… What do you think? Good night, my sister. And Roni, I forgot to tell you something important today: I love you very much.'

31
The Mystery of the Pacifier and the Scar

On Shabbat, Grandpa Gidi, Grandma Aliza and I went to visit Bilhah again. She's happy about the visit, and has even baked *kiplach* for us. Bilhah's now sitting opposite us. Today she looks much better than she did before.

We sit, drink tea and eat the tasty biscuits. Their fragrance and the sugar that she has put on them remind me of forgotten things. They remind me of the taste from Reiseleh's house. Even though I was really little, I remember the tastes and smells.

'*Nu*, so what's happening, Roni?' Bilhah asks. 'How are you getting on?'

'Truthfully, I'm not getting on at all. I'm waiting for the pages that Yosef promised to send me. I also need to look at the disk that Yoav brought me, and Naama brought me material from the camp in Atlit. But I want to hear the rest of your story most. You're a primary source for things. I'm impatient for this.'

Bilhah smiles.

'So where did we stop? Ah, yes, I went back home to the kibbutz, and told my husband, Chaim, about Shoshana. That very day, Chaim sat down to write letters: he wrote to everyone he knew in the hachsharah and in the hotel in Bratislava. "What do I have to lose? The price of the stamp at most. But maybe this way we will find our lost brothers," he said. One of the addressees was Mittyu Grinfeld.

'I wrote also. I decided to write to Shoshana at Atlit to encourage her. I was happy to receive a letter back from her two weeks later.'

Bilhah has done her homework. She immediately takes out a letter from a bag next to her and gives it to me. I spread out the folds of the letter. I don't understand a word of it.

'Bilhah, I don't know Czech. Would you read us the letter?'

Bilhah smiles her pleasant smile. She starts to read one line after another. First in Czech, and then she translates into Hebrew.

15 December 1940

You have no idea how much you helped me with that visit of yours. You scattered all the fog that surrounded me. You gave me advice about how to go on. Two days after you left, early on Thursday morning, I sat and wrote letters to whoever I thought might be in Mauritius. I hope the letters will reach their destination, and especially the letter I wrote to Mittyu. I hope he's there.

In the afternoon, the British officer, Simon, is supposed to come. I wait for him expectantly.

The chocolate you brought me is giving me much strength, and the juicy oranges too. I miss you. Please, write to me. Your words are healing for my illness.

I love and thank you for everything.

Please give my greetings to Chaim and kisses to little Yiftach.

Yours, Shoshana

'I was so happy that Shoshana was starting to recover, and I answered her at once. Sometime later, I got another letter from her. It had been sent on 29 December of that same year, about a month after the *Piatria* sank.'

Shalom to you, Bilhah,

Thank you again for the encouraging letter you sent me, and thank your Chaim who is helping to find our mutual friends.

Do you remember Simon, the British officer? He came exactly at noon, as he promised, and gave me an envelope. He said that there was a letter in it and he asked me to hide it. I put the envelope into my brassiere. My heart was entirely engrossed in my baby, and other things did not interest me.

I got in his jeep. There was a British nurse in the jeep and the three of us went to Haifa. All the way I was deep in thought: *will I find my Gidi? Is he alive?* Simon and the nurse didn't speak to each other very much either. They seemed sad to me. We were all engrossed in our own thoughts.

We reached a small hospital and found three injured immigrants there – two men and one woman. The woman had been on the *Atlantic*. I tried to get a little information from her, if she had seen an abandoned baby, but no, she hadn't. She was completely confused and didn't know anything, so she said in a whisper, as though speech were beyond her strength.

We continued looking. We reached the children's ward. I asked whoever came across my path: A baby. Small. Blue eyes… People gave me compassionate looks. Perhaps they thought I had gone mad. But no, they had not heard a thing about a small blue-eyed boy. My disappointment was immense. I could not stop the tears that came uncontrollably. Simon and the nurse bowed their heads.

'So what now?' I asked.

'We'll go to another hospital. There is one on Carmel.'

I feared another disappointment. When we arrived, I hurried straight to the children's ward.

I looked around me with wide eyes. Many cribs stood next to each other along the walls, small children and babies in them. Bilhah, you cannot imagine how tense I was. I went from crib to crib and my eyes looked here and there, right and left. I saw babies with scratches, some of them covered in sores, others with raw skin. They all slept. They must have been given a lot of medicine. I looked at their faces, but my Gidon I did not find. I felt the desperation rising in my throat and threatening to choke me.

The cry of a baby came from the end of the room. There, far away, stood a crib I had not checked. I went to it and looked closely at the baby lying there. He was covered in wounds and bruises. His eyes were closed and his skin was raw. I touched him. With great difficulty he opened his eyes, but when he did I saw that they were the colour of the sky. My heart leapt, but I still wasn't sure. I continued to look at him. Suddenly I saw a thread sticking out from under the cloth that covered him. I drew out the thread, and held the pacifier in my hand. Yes, this was my Gidi's pacifier. The old, white, tattered pacifier he loved. I fainted.

When I awoke, I saw the British nurse leaning over me. Simon stood to one side. It seemed to me that he wiped away a tear. I rose. I was shaking from weakness and joy together. I gathered the baby to me and held him tight. He tried to burrow his head into my chest, but the source of milk had gone dry. I looked at him for a long time. His eyes were blue, but there were yellow circles around his pupils. What was that?

The duty nurse came in. She looked at me from head to foot, and then asked if I was his mother.

'Yes, I am Shoshana Grinfeld. This baby is Gidon Grinfeld. Yes, this is my boy,' I told her with no small amount of pride.

The nurse smiled, but immediately added that I could not take him with me because he was very ill. 'He has jaundice, and he has been badly injured. We had to stitch the deep cut in his neck. We did not believe he would live.'

A long silence fell between us. She was the one to break it.

'He's lucky. You're lucky too. A German-speaking man brought him here. He was on the *Atlantic*. The baby was brought, bleeding heavily, salt-burned and unconscious. He was dressed in a blue suit, tattered and stiff with seawater. We were sure he would not even survive the night, but to our surprise, he recovered, and when we put him into a warm bath, he opened his eyes.'

'So when can I take him?'

'His situation is improving every day. This baby has learned to survive. He melts in the bathwater. He loves water, apparently. I wonder why?' said the nurse, and smiled a goodhearted smile. 'Perhaps in another week you can take him home.'

My eyes met hers. 'I have no home,' I said to her. 'I have a detention camp.'

That is it, my dear Bilhah. I have not yet heard from Mittyu. Nor from my sister or from Jutyu. I hope for the best. Rut, the young girl in my hut, helps me very much. I'm still weak, but my condition is improving all the time.

Do you remember what you told me when we met? 'After the winter comes the spring…'

I'm starting to believe this.

Kisses to you, your husband, and of course, to little Yiftach.

With love, Shoshana

Grandpa Gidi wipes his blue eyes with the handkerchief in his hand. Grandma Aliza is very moved as well. And I, I cling to my grandmother and cover my eyes. Yes, I'm already grown up, but I can't stop, and now I also am crying.

The mystery of the pacifier and the mystery of the scar have been solved, and my Grandpa Gidi is Gidi the baby. But one mystery still needs to be solved: where is the name 'Grinfeld' from? Grandpa Gidi's family name is Ramati.

The names of those in the women's camp at Atlit (from the green notebook written by Aviva Eschel). Marked: Gideon Scheiner

32
First Home in the Homeland

Bilhah looks exhausted.

'I'm going to bring something to drink,' she says, and Grandma Aliza gets up also and comes back from the kitchen with a tray in her hands. Bilhah sits down and sips from the cup before her. Now she looks more comfortable. Again she opens the bag next to her and takes out one more letter. As we are sipping from our cups she reads what is written.

Shalom to you, my dear Bilhah,

Yesterday I took Gidon from the hospital. We are both now in the camp at Atlit. Can you imagine how happy I am? In spite of the disgraceful conditions, the crowding, the terrible cold, and not knowing what tomorrow will bring, I'm happy. My Gidi is with me, and he even smiles at me. After my horrible despair, suddenly I find the boy.

Bilhah, I did not imagine life in the Land this way. When I lay exhausted and despairing in the ship, Mittyu sat next to me and spoke to me. He promised me a small house, a bit of grass, much light, and blue sky. And here there is barbed wire, narrow beds, terrible crowding, British policemen watching everyone closely. But enough. I don't want to complain. At least Gidon is with me. He has recovered from his jaundice, and the scar in his neck is slowly healing. I know the sun will rise tomorrow.

Do you remember I told you about a British nurse who joined us? She came to our shed and whispered in my ear that Simon is in jail. Interesting. Why and what for?

Letters are starting to arrive from Mauritius. Some of the women in our shed have already received letters from there. I'm still waiting.

Take care of yourself, dear Bilhah, and of your family. After all, you are all the family I have here.

With love, Shoshana

'That is the whole story, Roni. You should know that your Grandma Reiseleh, your great-grandmother, was a true hero. For nine months she was incarcerated in the camp at Atlit. When she was told that she would be released, she wrote me a joyful letter. I looked all over for it in order to show it to you, but I didn't find it. In any case, Chaim and I went to Atlit to take her and bring her to us. This was in the height of summer, in August. It was very hot that day, really blazing. Shoshana stood at the gate and waited for us. Gidon the baby was in her arms, and next to her was a brown suitcase with "Grinfeld" written on it in white letters.

'Reiseleh looked happy. She smiled and said that she had received a letter from Mittyu. Her sister and Yosef and Jutyu had also written to her at Atlit. She was sure that it would only be a matter of time until she saw her Mittyu and the rest of the family again.

'We took the bus as far as Tel Aviv, from Tel Aviv to Petach Tikva, and from there we took a wagon hitched to an old horse as far as the kibbutz. We had a one-roomed hut in the kibbutz. We shared it with Shoshana and the baby. My Chaim, may his memory be a blessing, who worked then in the kibbutz's carpentry workshop, made Gidon a beautiful cradle. I decorated it with a painting of sweet baby chicks and put a soft blanket in it. Gidon slept the sleep of the just in the new cradle. He always looked as though he were smiling in his sleep. We fell in love with him from the minute we saw him. A strong connection was forged between Shoshana and me, as though we were sisters.

'When Grandpa Mittyu passed away, when he was eighty-two, I felt I had lost a brother. And when Grandma Reiseleh passed away three months after him, I felt that I had lost a sister and a good friend. I miss these two heroes so much. I cannot believe that they are no longer among us.'

Bilhah is very moved. I go over to her and give her a strong hug, and whisper in her ear: 'You are truly great. You're my grandmother too… Thank you for everything.'

33
Annina

Grandma Aliza telephones excitedly: 'Roni, you won't believe this. Yesterday we went to meet some of the *Patria* survivors at the Navy Museum in Haifa. It's the seventieth anniversary of the sinking. We met adults there and old people as well, who brought albums, photos and letters. We talked with a seventy-year-old man named Uri. He told us that he was born on the *Atlantic*, and that his midwife, whose name is Annina, lives on the Kfar Ruppin kibbutz. We're going to meet her soon. We've set a time for this Shabbat. Would you like to come?'

'Of course I would, Grandma. Meet a woman who was with my great-grandparents on the ship? It'll be exciting.'

When we reach the kibbutz, we telephone Annina. She asks us to wait by the cafeteria. A few minutes later she comes on her electric scooter. She is a very elderly woman, and her Czech accent reminds Grandpa Gidi of his parents. She looks at us very attentively, particularly at Gidon. Her lined face shines, and she smiles at us warmly. We follow the scooter to her simple house, standing among deciduous trees. There are many stones in her front garden, and each is a different size and colour. 'Each stone here has a story,' Annina smiles at us. 'But you haven't come for stone stories, have you?' We enter her well-kept house, which is full of pictures, interesting stones and fallen vine leaves she has stuck on the windowpanes. I think to myself, *what an interesting curtain Annina has made for herself...* A warm cake is on the table, fragrant like the orchards, along with photo albums Annina has prepared beforehand.

We look at a few photos, until we see a photo of the camp in Bratislava. Annina tells us: 'I was in this camp for a few months. I lived in a long shack with many other women. I did any job I was given. It wasn't easy. But we all knew that in a short time we would receive the certificates and immigrate to the Land. There were small joys as well. What, for instance? I remember one couple who stole my heart: two people, he tall and imposing, and she a real beauty who was heavily pregnant. When I heard that a son had been born to them, I went with a friend and we bought a blue suit for the baby with the little money we had. We entered the shack where the new mother lived. She was so happy when she saw the gift we had brought for the baby. Her blue eyes welled up with joy.

'I looked at the baby, and he looked at me with his sea-blue eyes. It truly was a wonderful moment amidst the evil enveloping the world.'

'What was the baby's name?' asks Grandpa Gidi.

'Gidon. I remember that clearly. They called the baby by that name, after the biblical Gideon.'

'Annina,' says Grandpa Gidi, and his voice is cracked. 'This baby now sits in front of you. Ima told me of the first gift I received in the camp. Yes, she told me of a blue suit she put on me when we boarded the *Atlantic* on the way to Israel. In that same suit also...' Gidon cannot go on telling the story.

With shaking hands he takes a photo of his mother and father in their youth out of an envelope. Annina looks at the photo closely, and then at Gidon with big eyes that shine with excitement. 'This is it, now we've closed the circle… yes, this is the beautiful couple, and you… you…'

Annina cannot go on either.

34
A New Identity

I go back to the cassette player. The cassette stays in its place, and now I hear Grandpa Mittyu speaking.

Having no other choice, we became accustomed to the camp and its conditions. It was impossible to escape, although this idea came into the heads of many of those in prison there. It was surrounded by a high wall, and the guards stood alert at the gates twenty-four hours a day. All that was left for us was to simply work. We all did our best to make life there as normal as possible. We wrote many letters: to relatives in the Land, to friends on kibbutzim, to acquaintances in city and in village, to Atlit, and to Europe.

I wrote to my father and mother at Ungvar. One of the letters reached them, and I even received a response from them. It had been written in March 1942. I was excited to see my father's precise handwriting. Ima also wrote a few lines. Abba wrote that they had made all the necessary preparations in order to get an exit visa from Czechoslovakia, and even had packed up their suitcases. My father, my mother and my sister were waiting for the signal to leave, and I expected further information from them, from Ungvar or after they were already on their way. I missed them so much. The salty taste of Ima's tears is still on my tongue mixed with the taste of the *kiplach* she had baked for us for the journey. I waited impatiently to see my father, the respected man beloved of all, Ima, and Helinka, my beautiful sister.

We all continued to search for a solution to our situation on the island. We met many times in the evenings to think together about what could be done to leave this prison. This camp was not our destination when we boarded the Atlantic. In one of the meetings someone came up with a brilliant idea – to turn to the Czech consulate in South Africa and offer ourselves for service in the Czech army. Why, we were Czech subjects and it was right that we participate in the war effort to destroy the Nazis and their collaborators. And indeed, we turned to the consulate and were given an affirmative answer. Acting quickly, eighty of us joined the Czech army, and in a few days we were dressed in the uniform of the Czech Legion that fought alongside the British against the German army that had already reached North Africa.

We left the island in the summer of 1942 in ships sailing through the Red Sea, and reached Egypt.

Again the cassette stops. What has happened this time? The ribbon is finished. What now? How will I know what happened next? I am a bundle of nerves. My mother is always telling me that I need to learn to calm myself down: 'It's impossible to think when one is nervous or frustrated.'

So I say to myself, 'Roni, calm down. Enough. Your frustration won't bring a solution.'

I go outside. Right then, Grandma Aliza comes into our garden. She suggests that I go with her to the pool. Grandma and her ideas. I refuse, but she insists. I've already done my homework, so why not? I put on my bathing suit, stuff everything I need into a bag and we are on our way to the pool.

The water is pleasant. I give myself up entirely to its touch.

'Ronchu, what's making you angry this time?'

How does Grandma know how to read my mood? She always hits the bullseye.

'It's really annoying. It's the paper I'm writing. When it's most exciting, I get stuck.'

'Where are you stuck now?'

'The cassette ended right when I heard that Mittyu was going to Egypt dressed as a Czech soldier.'

Grandma splashes water on me and laughs. I splash water back at her and say, 'Why are you laughing, Grandma? Instead of helping me, you take me to the pool and laugh? Gosh, you don't understand me either.'

'Come, Roni. Let's go out get out of the water. I have something for you.'

We sit on comfortable lawn chairs by the pool. The sun gently strokes my body, and Grandma takes delicacies out of her bag. Swimming has given me an appetite. An orange from their garden peels itself in Grandma's quick hands.

'Roni, Grandpa Gidi will be happy to tell you what happened in Egypt. He won't try to escape from this episode! You know how much Grandpa Gidi loves history, and Grandpa Mittyu must've told him much about that time. Why, it is so natural that a father should tell his son such heroic stories.'

When we come back to Grandma's house, Grandpa Gidi is happy, as usual, to see me. He always has a big smile on his face and his eyes look happy when he sees me at the door. He hugs me.

'Now, Grandpa, you must help me finish my "roots" project. The cassette ended right when Grandpa Mittyu was telling about getting to Egypt as a Czech soldier. I don't have any more information.'

Grandpa Gidi smiles. He calls me into his study. He has a bookcase full of books there. He takes one book off the shelf: *The Young Pioneers in Karpathoros*. The book was printed in 1984. Some of the members of the movement wrote their memoirs. Grandpa gives me the book and I page through it. I see that also Grandpa

Mittyu and Grandma Reiseleh wrote their memoirs in this book. This is an excellent source.

We are now sitting with the book and reading:

> The volunteers for the Czech army reached Egypt. We were trained there for anti-aircraft fighting. This training went on for three weeks. Afterwards we were transferred to the Land, no less. Our excitement was great. Here, here at last we have reached Israel. Two years after the *Patria* had been sunk.

'And how did Grandpa Mittyu meet Grandma and the baby?' I ask.

'Slowly, slowly Roni. Again you're jumping to the end. Patience.'

We go on reading:

> Italian planes have attempted to strike the refineries in Haifa countless times. These refineries were built by the British, and my friends and I were stationed not far from them, to give a warning and even fire on enemy planes if they tried to approach. My job was important, but I felt that I was doing the work for a foreign army. Why, in Israel we had the Haganah and the Palmach. I was not at peace with being a Czech soldier in Haifa, far away from my friends in the Pioneer movement and the *hachsharah*, and it was hardest for me that I was far away from Shoshana and my baby, who must already be two years old.
>
> One day I met Shlomo, a childhood friend from Czechoslovakia, in Haifa. Shlomo had joined the Jewish Brigade with the intention of fighting the Nazis and their collaborators, and had come to the city. He advised me to desert, and in order to convince me said that many others were doing so and joining the Jewish forces. There was much work to be done: We must help the illegal immigrants to reach the land, to receive and absorb them here, to help found the kibbutzim and build houses. He again suggested that I desert. Just run away. And the sooner the better.

Grandpa Gidi falls silent. I am thinking in the meantime about what would be the right thing to do, but Grandpa interrupts my train of thought. He continues reading.

Shlomo suggested that I join their forces and enlist in the Haganah. He told me what Tabenkin, our guide, used to say: 'Wherever these boys should come from, they are not deserters, but rather making *aliyah* to Israel in any way possible.'

I thought about these things, and came to the conclusion that he was right. This was in fact our goal – to make *aliyah* to Israel, build it, fight alongside our brothers, to be with our family.

I close the book. I see Grandpa Gidi moving restlessly in his chair. Maybe now he'll explain some things to me?

'So Grandpa Mittyu deserted? How?'

By this question I feel that I have opened the dam. Grandpa Gidi begins: 'Grandpa Mittyu and a few other friends decided to desert. In the dead of night they escaped the camp in Haifa, and by hidden ways reached the Givat HaShloshah kibbutz. Grandpa knew that his Shoshana was there. He had received letters from her and from Bilhah and Chaim Kaminer. Under cover of darkness he entered the kibbutz and knocked on Chaim and Bilhah's hut door. Ima saw him at last, after two long years of waiting.'

'Grandpa, you can't remember the sinking of the ship?'

'Of course I don't remember the ship. But I do remember the day my father came. I woke up from sleep. I cried so much when I saw this strange man. He was big, dressed in strange clothes, dishevelled, dirty and frightening. He hugged my mother for a long time and Ima cried.'

'What, you didn't recognize your own father? Actually, that's a stupid question. You were only two and a half years old, right?'

'No, I didn't recognize that strange man. I was afraid of him. When he drew near to me, I began to cry and shouted: "Go, go, go away."'

'Ima tried to pacify me and said that this was Abba, this was Abba Mittyu, but I continued to cry bitterly and it was hard for me to calm down. When at last I did, I went back to my wooden bed, curled up in a blanket and tried to sleep. Suddenly we heard vehicles. I saw my father jump out of the window barefoot. I was afraid.

'Policemen from the Czech army surrounded the kibbutz in their vehicles. They had come to search for the deserters, for those who wanted to join the Haganah instead of serving their own army. Abba and his friends succeeded in escaping towards the field. The policemen went from house to house. They came into our room and found a Czech soldier's shoes. Abba had not been able to put them on before he ran away. This was enough to spur the soldiers on to continue their search. They searched the entire farm – the yard, the cow shed, the chicken run – but they did not find the deserters. Before they left they promised to return.

'And in fact for many days afterwards they continued to annoy the kibbutz people with their searches, and Abba and his friends were obliged to run from place to place, until they reached Ramat Hakovesh. For a week they hid there in the orchards. In order to keep himself from being identified, Abba cut his hair, changed his clothes, and even his last name. He received a new identification card.'

'What? Why?'

'Because he and his friends were afraid of getting caught. They knew they were likely to be put on trial for desertion and be sent to jail. So they decided to change their names. In his new identification card he was called Moshe Ramati, and not his true name, Mittyu Grinfeld.'

'Why Ramati?'

'Because he reached Ramat Hakovesh, the Conqueror's Plateau, and the "Ramat" became Ramati.'

'Now I understand. Now I understand why your family name isn't Grinfeld.'

'So my father came back to Givat HaShloshah with a new appearance and a new identity and from that time on we were not separated. I grew used to him. During those first days he joined Chaim and worked with him in the carpentry workshop. The first thing he made there was a rocking horse. Here, look at this picture. Here I am, riding this horse.'

I look at the picture hanging on the wall. A small boy, light-haired and with beautiful eyes rocking on a wooden horse.

'I was happy to gallop on the horse my father had made for me, but Abba did not stay with us for long. He joined a group that was going to found a kibbutz in the south, the Negev, and by the summer of 1944, in kibbutz Gvar'am, the house Abba had built was already standing. A little house with a red roof, and around it a small grassy garden. It had a flowerbed on one side, and the sun painted the petals with a rainbow of colours.'

'But Grandpa, now you're Gidi Ramati. And the name "Grinfeld"? You're the one who needs to continue the line and protect the roots, right?'

'That's true. That's an excellent question, and it bothered me for a long time. I keep the name "Grinfeld", and even sign that way. But if you want to meet someone whose name it really is, we should go to visit him in Ashkelon this coming Shabbat."

35
Petr

I was very excited to meet Petr. I knew Noa would be there too.

Petr sits opposite us, and Noa sits next to him. She smiles at me. I answer her with a very particular smile. No one knows about the connection between us. When the time is right maybe I will tell my mum. I tell her all my secrets, and this is a new one. So now Grandma Aliza, Grandpa Gidi and I sit in Petr's humble house in Ashkelon. Many photographs are on the piano, and he has many albums as well, with thank you letters from boys who were with him in Auschwitz and in the death camps in Poland. Petr looks old, perhaps even elderly, even though he is no older than Grandpa Gidi.

I look at this man, and remember his face dimly. Yes, he was one of the mourners at Grandpa Mittyu's funeral after he passed away. I don't remember what he said, but I do remember that his words moved me very much, and he ended with: 'My brother, my own brother…' But this memory only complicates things in my head.

Petr brings out a photo album. He shows us a photo of a big house. A house, two storeys high, with a roof covered in snow.

'This is the house I grew up in,' Petr says, 'after I came out from "there"…'

'Where did you come out from?' I ask.

Petr has beautiful eyes, but his jaw is a little malformed and he is lacking a few teeth. His back is stooped and wrinkles line his cheeks.

'My grandchildren also did a "roots" project,' he tells me. 'They didn't understand either. Or more rightly: they didn't believe it. Yes, the things that happened in this war are inconceivable. The human brain cannot think them, and it's precisely for this reason that it is important to tell whoever wants to listen.

'I was the youngest child in Auschwitz. I was not sent to the gas chambers. Why? Because I had the luck of having a twin sister. Twins were taken for experiments. I was a "laboratory rat" for Dr Mengele. He conducted experiments on twins' bodies. He even checked the vocal cords. He wanted to learn about the height, the head size of twin siblings, about blood type – anything to advance science…'

Silence falls in the room. Petr is sunk in his past. He is "returning" there. I wait. The quiet is heavy, intense.

'Pepiczek. So I was called by all the twins who were with me, all male, of course. I had not seen my twin sister, Marta, since I was torn away from my mother. My mother tried to hold on to me, but they were stronger than her. I screamed at the top of my lungs. So did Marta. My redheaded sister, Emilia, who was older than we were, cried aloud.

'Many people were there, and were divided into two groups. I was sent to the left. I was short and thin. I looked back and saw my mother. She shouted to me: "Pepiczek, don't forget. You are a Jewish boy from Prague." And she called again. I wanted to run to her. I was pushed forward roughly. I did not stop crying. There were many twins in the huge barracks they led me to: children, youths, adults, all frightened. Every day more and more twins were added to the barracks, and others simply vanished.

'One day a dwarf came into the barracks. An adult dwarf. He was my height. His name was Laiusz. He was a painter. Laiusz was in my bunk. This was great luck because his coat was too big for him, and we could both cover ourselves with it at night. It was so cold in Auschwitz, especially during the nights. A German officer was there, smelling of soap, who used to come to our barracks so that Laiusz could paint him. Only Laiusz and I remained in the barracks after all the men had gone out early in the morning to work, or had been taken for experiments. So the whole time that the German sat for the "painter", I lay quietly under the bunk. I did not even dare to breathe, I was so afraid of him. When Laiusz would finish painting, the German would give Laiusz candy.

'When I was taken to the green room [Mengele's experiment room], he was there, the officer who smelled of soap. He gave me an injection and all my body hurt. Once when I was brought back from there, I could not move. My back hurt very much and my legs were immobilized. I don't know what was done to me there. To this day I suffer from back pain, because of being Mengele's laboratory rat.

'The only clothing I had was a thin striped nightgown. When it was cold I would curl up in rags other twins had left behind in the barracks when they went to work. They were laying train tracks into the camp at Auschwitz, so that the coming convoys would reach right to the entrance of the gas chambers and crematoriums.'

Petr tells us that it was 27 January 1945 by the time the Russians liberated whoever was left in the extermination camp at Auschwitz. The cursed Nazis had been defeated, and the Russian army opened the gates of hell. The few who survived were set free, but where would they go?

Petr is silent for a long time. I cannot keep silent and ask: 'Who was with you? Where did you go? You were so small. How are you connected to the name "Grinfeld"?'

'Roni, I'm a little tired. Perhaps some other time?'

Noa gets up. She comes over to me and gives me the 'roots' project she has written.

'I am relying on you to keep it safe,' she says.

I feel I am blushing. I thank her and take the album she gives me. We go home. I am curious to read what already has been written about Pepiczek in Noa's project. The next day, immediately after I have done all my homework, I sit and page through her project. It is very in-depth. She has written a lot about her grandmother, Olga, Petr's wife who has passed away. I continue leafing through until I reach the story of what had happened to Petr.

> I left the camp with some other twins. I had an adult friend named Guttmann. He took hold of my hand and dragged me out of the gate. It was very crowded there. People were pushing towards the open gate and wanted to leave. My arm was almost torn from its place.
>
> I lost Guttmann. I heard him shouting, 'Pepiczek, Pepiczek,' but I could not reach him in the thick of the crowd. I walked among the many who were leaving and fell down in the snow. I could not rise. The snow fell, people stepped over me, and I fell asleep covered in snow. I had strange dreams there. I saw my mother, she smiled to me and stroked my cold cheek. I felt someone stroking my cheeks and heard him speaking to me in Hungarian, and then in German, and at last in Czech. He asked my name. It was hard for me to open my eyes. They were covered in snow. When I was able to open them a little I saw a middle-aged man. I was afraid. I did not want to tell him my name. At the camp, when I was asked for my name and I said 'Pepiczek', I was slapped across the face. I told him only the number that was tattooed on my arm: A–4953. This man picked me up, held me to his chest, embraced me in his arms and wept. I did not understand why he was crying.
>
> 'My name is Pepiczek. Don't cry,' I said to him, and was no longer afraid of him.
>
> The man did not stop crying, but I also saw a smile on his face.

'My name is Shmuel. I'm Shmuel Grinfeld. Now you're with me. Don't worry,' he said.

Shmuel Grinfeld? Why, Shmuel is Mittyu and Jutyu's father. He is the one who found Pepiczek in the snow? I'm very curious. I continue reading:

> He walked slowly, holding me to his chest. I felt that he had no strength. He continually looked around him; he looked for Margot, his wife, and Helinka, his daughter. No, he was not sure that they had been sent to Auschwitz. We continued slowly, the wooden shoes on his feet making holes in the deep snow. He had no strength to continue walking. He set me down and said: 'Now we will walk together. You're big now.' And I, my legs could not carry me. I was so tired and hungry.

Ima comes over to me, holding a plate with luscious fresh fruit in her hand: slices of apples, oranges, and red strawberries. She looks at me and sees the tears in my eyes. She sits down next to me, holds me warmly and leans my head on her shoulder. Ima is next to me and I have a father, a brother and sisters, a home, and a plate full of good things. Pepiczek had nothing.

Ima asks me to go outside to get some air. I go out. I see all my friends there and they are running, jumping, skipping, on roller skates, riding bicycles, bouncing balls. I look at them and think: *How good we have it. I have friends. They are happy and joyful, and each one has a place to return to.*

Only three days later I go back to Noa's 'roots' project.

> I told Shmuel that the last words my mother had said to me were: 'You are a Jewish boy from Prague.' Grandfather Shmuel and I returned to Prague and tried to find my home. We walked the streets of the city and searched. I did not remember where it stood. I was about four years old when we were driven out of our house. We asked people in the street, but no one knew a family where the mother was called Helena, the sister was called Marta, her twin was

Petr, and there was another red-haired sister called Emilia. I did not remember my father's name nor my family name. All the searches were for nothing. We did not find anything.

Shmuel Grinfeld took me to Ungvar, which was called Uzhgorod after the war. We came to a big house with two storeys, with a sign on its front: Restaurant and Coffeehouse. The first storey had been a coffeehouse and restaurant, and on the second floor was the spacious apartment where Shmuel Grinfeld's family had lived.

The house was neglected and part of it had been destroyed. Shmuel and I began the task of restoring it – restoring the house and restoring the coffeehouse. One morning Shmuel woke me up even before dawn and we both went out to the garden. Shmuel dug next to a rosebush and took out a box.

'Pepiczek, it's so lucky that I hid money and jewels here before we were taken away,' he said. With this money Shmuel bought all that was necessary: he painted and repaired, and I of course helped him. Some days later, he opened the coffeehouse and hired three gypsy violinists. The Hungarian gypsy music drew passers-by inside. People came into the coffeehouse to enjoy a pleasant atmosphere and to taste homemade biscuits. Shmuel managed the place, and I was his assistant.

Grandfather Shmuel did not, for one second, stop waiting for his wife Margot and his daughter Helinka. He continued searching for them tirelessly. Sometimes he would tell me about Jutyu and Mittyu, his two sons, who were apparently in Israel, but he could not say where they were exactly. He promised to continue and search for my family as well.

'You are my child and I am your father. And if we find your family, then I'll continue to be your father. If you would like it…'

Such a good man was Shmuel Grinfeld, my new father. He lavished much love on me. But no, we did not find anyone from the family. Only Shmuel and I were left. Shmuel the father, and I, his son.

Many guests came to the coffeehouse. The gypsies who played the violin were a magnet. Grandfather Shmuel and I worked hard. I kneaded dough, Grandfather baked sweet biscuits, and the wonderful smell filled the whole coffeehouse. But sadness could still be seen on Grandfather Shmuel's face. He kept waiting.

One morning a party of Russian soldiers came to the coffeehouse, an unruly party who wanted to get drunk. They drank and drank, cursed and went wild, and Grandfather Shmuel served them as they demanded. I stood next to him, afraid. I was afraid of any soldier. I always shivered when I saw soldiers.

There were few people in the coffeehouse. The musicians had not arrived yet. The soldiers got up and went to the door. Grandfather Shmuel went over to them and said: 'You forgot to pay.' And then… then one of the drunk soldiers took out a pistol. I heard five shots. I saw Grandfather Shmuel fall. He lay in a pool of blood. I ran to him, went down on my knees and looked in his face, shook him and screamed: '*Tata! Tata!*' But Tata did not answer.

Grandfather Shmuel died.

He did not die in Auschwitz. The forced labour there did not vanquish him. He died in his own house, in the coffeehouse he owned, shot by drunken soldiers. The man who had survived hell was murdered for nothing, for no reason.

At his funeral, the gypsies played the melodies Grandpa Shmuel had loved. The sounds of the violins mixed with my own weeping. I wept aloud. Again I am alone. Again I have no one in the world. After the funeral, neighbours took me into their house.

I close Noa's 'roots' project. I am devastated. It is hard for me to digest what I have just read. The sight of the coffeehouse stands before my eyes, and the small boy, who again is left without a family…

Some weeks later Helinka, Shmuel and Margot's daughter, came to the neighbours' house. She had survived. How beautiful she was, but so thin and very frightened. She also had gone through Auschwitz. She took me with her and I became her son. We were waiting for Margot. Perhaps she would surprise us and come?

When Helinka was married to Yankeleh Greenberger, I became Petr Greenberger. Since then he became my father. But first of all I am Grinfeld. I've kept this name. In any case, I didn't know my own family name.

Grinfeld is also my children's family name. I owe this to the man who was my guardian angel. Were it not for him, I would have frozen to death there in the snow.

Pepiczek found his true family name only when he was thirty-five years old. He came to the Lochamei HaGeta'ot kibbutz, and by the number tattooed on his arm he found that his family name was Kleinmann. He received documents, and these listed all his other family members, and the dates when all the experiments had been done on him and his sister in Auschwitz. Not one of his family had survived. He is doubtful concerning Marta's fate. Even today he holds fast to the hope that she is alive somewhere on the face of the earth.

For thirty years he searched for his name. Now he has an identification card, and there are three family names on it: Grinfeld, Greenberger and Kleinmann. The man with the three identities. What a great man.

Helinka, Mittyu and Jutyu's sister, survived the forced labour. She raised a beautiful family; she raised Pepiczek, and she and Yankeleh had two children of their own. She met Mittyu and Jutyu in Israel after many years of separation.

She passed away old and full of years, but the hard memories and the pain of losing all her family did not leave her till the day she died. Perhaps it is a great comfort that she left behind her three families: Pepiczek's family and the two families of her own children, who will be the connecting link in the chain of family generations.

36
Simon

This is it. I am taking great care about the ending of the paper. I will give my deep roots to my own children as a legacy. 'This melody is unstoppable…' I write in the last chapter.

The brown suitcase marked 'Grinfeld' is at our house. I mean to guard it and give it and all its contents to the children I will have when I am grown – the blue album, the pacifier, the letters and the photographs.

I empty the suitcase. I want to clean and wipe it, and make order in all the papers. Gingerly I shake the dust off it, put a little bit of talc on its sides, wipe the lid with a soft cloth, and put some balls of naphthalene in it so that the papers will be preserved.

Suddenly I see a bump between the side of the suitcase and the lining. It is as though the bump winks at me and says: 'Look at me.' I look at the frayed lining. I stick my hand between the lining and the side. There is paper inside. I take it out. It's very wrinkled. Slowly, carefully I spread the paper out with my fingers. I feel my heart beating strongly.

I look at the writing. I can read it: the letter is written in English. The date is faded, but the handwriting can still be read.

Dear Mrs Grinfeld,

I ask you, most earnestly, to destroy this letter immediately after you read it. I found your suitcase thrown among many other suitcases and items that were saved out of the *Patria*. I hope you will find some comfort in it.

I was sent to the detention camp at Atlit to guard the people who were brought here from the *Atlantic*, to guard all the ones that we were not able to transfer to the *Patria*. Everyone is to be exiled to Mauritius. I saw the name 'Grinfeld' in the men's list in the big barracks. I plan to get him out of there in order to prevent his exile. My plan is to bring him to one of the barracks close to yours, where all the ones who had been on the ship that sank have been gathered together.

All those who had been on the *Patria* will receive a pardon. They will stay at Atlit and eventually be freed. Not everyone together, but slowly, slowly they will all be released. They will stay in Israel. I want you to know that your husband is alive. I hope very much that you will soon find your baby also.

I know I am risking myself and my job here. But I must act according to my conscience. I know very well what it is to lose a family member. I lost touch with my dear wife, Rita, and to this day I hope that she is alive. And you, you so remind me of her.

My wife is Jewish. She came to London to study five years ago from a small village in Czechoslovakia. When I saw you for the first time here in the camp, I lost my breath. You so remind me of my wife.

Since I was married to her, we have lived in London. About a year ago she went to meet her sister Sheindele, who is married to Chaim Scheiner of Bushtina. They had a baby, Miriam, and my Rita wanted to see her sister and her first niece so much. I pleaded with her not to go, but she insisted. She promised that her journey to Czechoslovakia would be very short and that she would come back immediately. To my sorrow, the war trapped her there. She wrote to me that her way out was blocked and that she could not come back to London. She reached the Ulmitz *hachsharah* camp with her sister and the baby. From there she hoped to get to London with her sister, her husband and the baby. She believed that they would be able to escape from there, but it is more than a year now that I am waiting for a sign ... from her or from her family – but nothing. All my searching for her has not yielded any fruit. I have written letters, but no answer has arrived.

I joined the British army with the intention of fighting the Nazis and whoever helps them. To my sorrow, I was not sent to the battlefield, as I had hoped. Instead, I was sent here to assist in taking care of the Jewish illegal immigrants. I am getting into intolerable situations. I must obey orders. I'm a soldier, and I must obey orders, but I am doing everything I can in order to not lose my humanity...

Many times I act according to my conscience and against instructions, although I know I'm risking myself. I feel the refugees' pain and know well your anger against us because of my country's policies. It is a sorrow to me that we act this way. It utterly opposes my opinions and beliefs.

Please, do not judge me. I promise you to do everything, truly everything, to help your husband escape the exile.

With blessings,

Simon Harman, a man who cares

I read what is written and do not believe my eyes. I read from the beginning again. It seems that Grandma Reiseleh did not read the letter. She stuck it, apparently, into the side of the suitcase when she was looking quickly for a place to hide it. Perhaps she would have saved herself much worry and heartache if she had read it. For many days she waited for a sign of life from Mittyu, and the answer was in this letter. Simon wanted to help her. It is truly too bad that Reiseleh did not tell Simon that her maiden name was Scheiner.

According to the facts, Simon was not able to keep Mittyu from being deported to Mauritius. He also paid for the help he gave many illegal immigrants by being sentenced to jail. He was imprisoned, apparently, in the British jail in Acre.

I am thinking about Simon. A man acts according to the commands of his conscience, tries to stay human even in the hardest situations that result from war, and pays for it with his freedom.

That moment I give myself a new task – to try to find him and thank him in Reiseleh my great-grandmother's name, who is no more.

I tell the whole family about my revelation. Shiri has got the detective bug as well. She has promised to help me. According to our calculations, Simon is very old, if in fact he is still alive. How will we find out something about him?

Grandpa Gidi comes to our rescue. He turns to the 'Search Bureau for Missing Relatives' on the radio and goes on the broadcast. People are searching for their relatives till this day. He asks them to locate Simon and gives all the details he knows about him. At that same time he asks if they would also search for the man who took the baby out of Reiseleh's hands on the sinking ship. All Grandpa Gidi knows was that the man came from Vienna and was on the *Patria*. Grandpa Gidi has also joined my detective work, but unsuccessfully. We do not receive any response after the radio broadcast.

Grandpa Gidi has not found Simon or the Viennese man who saved him from drowning.

Shiri has already started with her own private detective work. She is asking Grandma Aliza many questions about her own roots. Grandma Aliza also has an exciting story about her family's 'Exodus from Egypt'. The truth is, I'm also already curious to hear her story.

But not now.

Glossary

Abba – father (informal)
Aliyah –is the immigration of Jews from the diaspora to the Land of Israel.
Challah – a braided bread which is eaten on the Sabbath.
Dreidel – a spinning top associated with the festival of Hanukkah.
Eretz Israel – the Land of Israel.
Ha'apala – the clandestine immigration to Eretz Israel during the British Mandate period.
Hachshara – preparation for Zionist youth.
Haganah – (the Defence) the underground army of the Yishuv (Jewish community).
Hora – an Israeli circle dance.
HaShem – 'the Name', a euphemism for God.
HaTikvah – (the Hope) is the national anthem of the State of Israel.
Ima – mother (informal)
Moshav – a cooperative village in Israel.
Minyan – the ten men required for public prayer in Judaism. It can also mean a prayer service.
Nu – (Yiddish) can be translated 'Well?' 'So?' 'Indeed!'

Palmach – was the elite striking force of the Haganah.

Palyam – the naval force of the Palmach.

Passover Haggadah – the Haggadah (telling) is the order of service for the Passover meal.

Rugelach – a pastry made by Ashkenazi Jews.

Shalom – peace, well-being. 'Shalom!' is a common greeting.

Shoah – (calamity) The murder of European Jews by the Nazis during World War Two. Hitler's "Final Solution".

Yishuv – Jewish Community